GIRL IN
NEED OF A
TOURNIQUET

MEMOIR OF A BORDERLINE PERSONALITY

MERRI
LISA
JOHNSON

SEAL PRESS

GIRL IN NEED OF A TOURNIQUET
Memoir of a Borderline Personality

Published by
Seal Press
A Member of the Perseus Books Group
1700 Fourth Street
Berkeley, California

Library of Congress Cataloging-in-Publication Data

Johnson, Merri Lisa.
  Girl in need of a tourniquet : memoir of a borderline personality / by
Merri Lisa Johnson.
     p. cm.
  ISBN 978-1-58005-305-1
  1. Borderline personality disorder. 2. Personality disorders.
I. Title.
  RC569.5.B67J64 2010
  616.85'852—dc22
                                        2009053856

9 8 7 6 5 4 3 2 1

Cover and interior design by Domini Dragoone
Printed in the United States by Edwards Brothers
Distributed by Publishers Group West

DEDICATION

To Stacey—

I love you like I love the sun.

CONTENTS

You look like a perfect fit

for a girl in need of a tourniquet.

But can you save me. . . .

—Aimee Mann, "Save Me"

A borderline suffers a kind of emotional hemophilia;

[s]he lacks the clotting mechanism needed to moderate

[her] spurts of feeling. Stimulate a passion,

and the borderline emotionally bleeds to death.

—Jerold Kreisman and Hal Straus,

I Hate You, Don't Leave Me:

Understanding Borderline Personality Disorder

AUTHOR'S NOTE

Most names have been changed.

The timeline has been compressed for clarity and pace.

UNSOLVED HEART

I GRADUATED COLLEGE the same week Lisa Lopes set her boyfriend's house on fire.

Her fans knew her as Left Eye. Her boyfriend, Andre Rison, played for the Atlanta Falcons. He had been out late. She had been drinking. "Things went from bad to worse," said *People* magazine. "Even before the fire, the couple had a combustive relationship." Left Eye didn't mean to burn the house down. She thought the fire would stay contained to the bathtub, she says, but the shoes burned hotter than expected.

I KNOW WHAT SHE MEANS.

I picture the fire roaring up from the roof of the mansion in a pink and orange flash, like the fireworks at Stone Mountain. I lived in a rental that year, a small box where I stored my own rage like torn photographs from my too-young marriage (nineteen) and my too-soon divorce (twenty), a crooked and poorly insulated house where mice walked boldly across the dining room table and the kitchen sprouted gray flowers of mold. I crawled from my bed at 5:00 AM on the morning of July 9, 1994, and opened my front door to watch the fire from my porch forty miles west of Atlanta. I stood on the tiny concrete square holding an unlit cigarette and looked up to see another woman's frustration flash above my head like a warning or a mirror.

I didn't really see the blaze from the fire.

I only wish I did. The truth is, I couldn't have.

Even if the Atlanta skyline had been visible in the dark countryside of western Georgia I would not have seen the distress signal on the horizon. Most likely I was sleeping or sexing a Sigma Nu or vomiting red and blue squares of vodka Jell-O.

Lisa Lopes poured lighter fuel on a bathtub full of tennis shoes and threw a lit match on top to punctuate her words—*I don't care anymore!*—and I didn't care anymore either. Five nights later I raged at the *would-have-been-ness* of my second wedding anniversary by working my first shift as a stripper at the Coronet Club on Roswell Road in Atlanta.

I WAS SETTING FIRES THAT YEAR TOO.
I WENT CRAZY THAT YEAR TOO.

I TRIED THERAPY. I TRIED COCAINE.

I STOPPED READING. I STOPPED MENSTRUATING.

I changed my name to Summer as if I were not a person but an endless stretch of white-hot days people long for and then wish away. If the fire Left Eye set had seared my wood-panel walls with words like EMOTIONAL HIJACKING or DISPROPORTIONATE REACTION, I would have been too distracted by my own depression to notice.

Eight years later Left Eye will die in a head-on collision and I will again be too absorbed by personal strife to pay attention to news of a celebrity death. I will be packing my books and clothes and knick-knacks, thinking about my new home in another state, hoping things will be better when I get there. I will be packing and crying, packing and getting drunk, packing and asking people to remind me not to call the married man I just broke up with. I will be consumed by thoughts of getting away. I will still believe the problem is outside me—a matter of being in the wrong place at the wrong time with the wrong people—and I will speak of these places and people and their wrongness with the same conviction Lisa Lopes speaks of evil spirits chasing her car across Honduras before the crash. My life story is structured by reckless reenactments of panic and flight.

I tend to veer off the road. I tend to overcorrect.

Skid. S — P — I — N. Tense up for the wreck.

I TELL THE STORY of being married at nineteen and divorced at twenty over and over.

I have been telling it for fifteen years. I have become less compulsive but for years I spared no detail. All I needed was a dark room and a glass of wine, and I rolled tape.

ACTION: I went to study abroad in France for a summer because a marriage that can't survive six weeks apart is not a marriage worth having. I would have been embarrassed to give up an opportunity to grow and learn and suck the marrow from life out of girlish insecurity. While I was gone my husband moved out. A lawyer drew up divorce papers. Kittens went feral in our apartment. I am unable to match the scenes of him leaving me with scenes from before I flew away to France.

BEFORE is the two of us eating the top portion of the wedding cake saved for a year in the freezer for luck. We lick frozen icing from our fingertips and feel blue about being apart for six weeks. *Maybe it will be unbearable. Maybe becoming fluent in French is not worth this pain.* Our eyes open wide. *Maybe we made a mistake.*

AFTER is me on the bedroom floor with my back against the wall and my face coming apart in my hands. I watch him move the contents of his dresser drawers to a duffle bag. He doesn't even look at me when I hiccup and yowl.

AFTER-AFTER is the long depression I misrecognize as missing my ex. I wade through the rush of NEGLECT and LOSS and SADNESS pouring through a hole in my hull. The abruptness changes me. I become angry. I seek pain out and shout at it.

I laughed at people who made promises to each other. I laughed at people who got hurt. *What did you expect?* I wanted to say. I muttered under my breath. *Fools.*

I had sex with a boy who dipped snuff. His tobacco-soaked fingers stung between my legs. I wondered if his fiancée ever complained. I pushed my body down harder and leaned into the wince. I said forbidden words like GODDAMN. I lost weight. I lost drive. I wore dark lipstick and black leather breakaway thongs that snapped at the hip. I pulled them off on stage, my narrow body a middle finger in the air. I said *god is dead.* I said *love is dead. The person I used to be,* I said, *she's dead too.* I drove away.

I FELL IN LOVE AGAIN FOUR YEARS LATER AND CRAFTED MY LIFE INTO A POEM FOR HIM.

The poem consisted of two words.

LOVE ME.

This lover became more project than partner and I sometimes wished him *poetcrippledead* in anger at his mixed signals. I worked obsessively to understand the two-sidedness of the relationship—how much I loved him, how much I wanted him to change—outlining piles of evidence to friends over drinks. I wanted them to help me figure out what was what.

HE LOVES ME

He invited me to spend a week with him in Argentina. He made my coffee sugary sweet every morning and brought it to me in bed. He said being with me made him want to thank a god he didn't even believe in. He held me closer than close during sex and whispered *Open your eyes, look at me* and when I did my heart rose up from my chest and became one with his.

HE LOVES ME NOT

He said living in the same town with his girlfriend would be close enough. Not in the same house. He didn't want another marriage. When I asked him if we were forever he just said *Don't start.* He sang Willie Nelson's "My Heroes Have Always Been Cowboys" over and over one night when he was drunk. He didn't even stop when I pretended to vomit in the toilet.

"What does this mean?" I moaned to my friends.

My need to understand these stories was strong enough to drive me past self-consciousness into counterphobic displays. Embarrassing moments spread like polaroids of my naked body on the table. I wanted to know how other people processed the changing light of a room in the face of uncertain affections.

"Have you ever considered therapy?"

The question jarred me. I learned the way of quiet isolation.

YEARS WILL PASS. Picture them like the pine dark shoulders of the interstate between my old house and the one where Lisa Lopes kept her lighter fluid. One night I will watch a documentary called *Last Days of Left Eye* to hear Lopes setting the record straight.

> *They tell it like I was just CRAZY DRUNK OUT MY MIND didn't know what I was doing and just for no reason decided to burn down a house. I NEVER SAID A WORD about what happened. But people were printing stories LIKE IT WAS THE GOSPEL TRUTH.*

Visibly pained by media images that portray her as a crazy person, an alcoholic, a danger to herself and to others, Left Eye brings out the backstory—the building frustrations in her relationship with Andre; the way she felt disrespected, abused, neglected, villainized; the way she tried to flip the script by going out with friends in a sexy dress and staying out till five in the morning; the way her mouth dropped open in surprise when she got home and he wasn't back yet.

> *I just stood there, she says.*
>
> *I was enraged. I was in a trance.*

THE REST OF THE STORY FROM THAT NIGHT
COMES IN FLASHES.

Hard words, fists, accusations, lighter fuel. Conflagration.

Her rage, shaped like a tub full of shoes on fire, burning hotter and hotter. I picture her gazing into a fiery blaze. My eyes lock on her eyes as the screen fades to grainy footage of Left Eye riding in the back of a police car on her way to the Fulton County Jail. Butterflies swoop and flutter in my stomach when I hear what she says.

Don't believe anything you hear.
Or half of what you see.

I know what she means.

I have frightened people. I have risked lives.

I have held lit matches in my hand and stared into the blue impulse. I have leapt through my lover's roof into a flaming orange sky. I have spoken of forever in tongues of fire. I have torn whole towns in two for love. I have courted insanity, crouching in the gap between what this moment feels like (*the smoldering fire fanned into the most logical flames*) and how it looks to other people (*the psychotic break of spontaneous combustion*). I can feel the sensation (*it burns*) of being called CRAZY when you feel WOUNDED and DESPERATE.

I could so easily have set a house on fire.

I could so easily have found myself behind bars.

"How you know?" Sula asked.

"Know what?" Nel still wouldn't look at her.

"About who was good. How you know it was you?"

"What you mean?"

"I mean maybe it wasn't you. Maybe it was me."

—Toni Morrison, *Sula*

I GREW UP believing RIGHT and WRONG were two separate dimensions of reality and anyone who tried hard enough could easily tell them apart. No matter how I fought to free myself of this painfully simple value system, life appeared to me in the form of a test. One question. Two answers. Two possible paths to two very different fates—the way of goodness and insight versus the way of badness and eternal confusion. I filled in a bubble with my number two pencil and erased it to fill in the other one. I darkened the circles and erased until the paper smudged and tore and I could no longer see the question.

I entered therapy in my early thirties and established a handful of urgent psychological goals. The main one was to stop living in the nervous state of reaction. I longed to stabilize my core identity and to withstand the pressure of other people's words, behaviors, moods, and perceptions. I wanted to be less easily thrown.

I HAVE BEEN writing *Girl in Need of a Tourniquet* for more than five years, a time period that coincided with my first sustained attempt not merely to understand but to change my habits of perception and reaction, to become more graceful and fair in my interpersonal relationships. Yet I resisted change. My resistance limited the memoir to mirror rather than lamp. I produced many versions of the same story—each one warped by defensiveness, wrapped in arrogance, worn thin by neurosis, and situated in the unpredictable ground of a volatile ego—and played musical chairs with its meaning.

It *was a book about heartbreak.* IT WAS A BOOK ABOUT OBSESSION. *It was a book about a woman who drove me crazy.* THE WOMAN WAS MY LOVER. The woman was my *mother.* The woman was ME.

No.

It was a book about vicious introjects, implicit memories, and relentless reenactments of trauma and recovery. IT WAS A BOOK ABOUT GENDER, POWER, AND NARRATIVE, ABOUT PERSONALITY, PAIR-BONDS, AND THE POLITICS OF DIAGNOSIS. *It was a book about Zen mindfulness, neural pathways, and family mysteries.* IT WAS A BOOK ABOUT SOUL-WRENCHING BLUES, BRIGHT RED SCREAMS, LOVE DOGS, GRIEF WORK, AND HAPPINESS FILLING THE LUNGS LIKE THE HOT WHITE RIOT OF GARDENIAS.

THE BOOK WAS NOT A BOOK BUT A SYMPTOM.

My words came out in the wrong dis/order. I couldn't make it write.

⸻

I sat up all night with a razor in my hand and did drugs with it. One line for the book. One line for me. I told the book terrible secrets, then felt weird (*too close too fast*) and slipped out the door while it slept. I got sick of the book and wanted it to move out. My newlywed spouse screamed at me to get over it. S/he said s/he hated the book. S/he said I couldn't bring it into our bed anymore. We had taken the manuscript as a third in unholy matrimony and s/he wanted the threesome to end. The book was all I talked about. S/he accused me of wanting to be with the book forever. *Maybe I should marry the book,* s/he said.

I worked through memories like weeping wounds. I wrote tedious accounts of petty conflicts and read them aloud to people. I removed layer after layer of rot.

I GOT SICK OF MYSELF. I WANTED ME TO MOVE OUT TOO.

I bored myself to tears with the daytime television drama of confrontation *(I've been wronged!)*. I winced at sluggish morning half-memories of wearing wrongness like a lampshade on my head *(I'm mentally ill!)*. The space between accusation and atonement is narrow as a kitchen chair. Writing the book felt like being tied to that chair. Constrained by familiar coils of narrative—THE COMPLAINT and THE CONFESSION—I wrote things I hated and said things I did not believe.

THE HOUSE OF MY SELF WAS ON FIRE.

MY THROAT WAS A BROKEN ARTERY.

BLOOD POURED INTO THE FLOOR.

I studied the lovely grain of the arrow in my body until I grew faint and slumped in my seat, finally able to quit fretting over the question of who was right (*maybe it was you!*) and who was wrong (*maybe it was me!*). I relinquished the whole idea of the question and stopped wearing circles in the carpet.

I GAVE UP.

I PRETENDED NOT TO CARE ABOUT THE STORY.

I PRETENDED I DIDN'T KNOW IT.

Days / weeks / months passed.

Finally I went to the story in a new way—without yelling or lying or crying over what remains unsolved—and sat with my hands loose in my lap.

I let go of something. I made room for something.

A TANGLE OF WORDS UNWOUND.

ATTACHMENT THIEF

STRANGE

1. SEX WITH A NEW SEXUAL PARTNER. . . .

3. SEX OUTSIDE YOUR CURRENT RELATIONSHIP.

—URBAN DICTIONARY

LAST NIGHT I dreamed I slept with a married colleague.

It is late summer and I am going to a meeting on campus, beginning my second year in a job at a small university near the beach in South Carolina. I smile into my coffee cup at the memory of imagined pleasure. Flashes of the dream come back to me as I am brushing my teeth. He pulls me toward him by the hips. We are in the back seat of a car somewhere. I straddle his lap and we laugh and laugh. We are sitting next to each other in a meeting, our hands side by side at the edge of our seats. He loops his pinky finger over my thumb and my whole body runs hot. I slow this snippet down in my imagination. I swish mouthwash from one side of my mouth to the other and stare at myself in the bathroom mirror.

Do I want to have an affair with this man?

IN A WAY, YES.

> I want to push my face into his tweedy shoulder, feel
> his hand on the back of my hair, inhale the scent
> of his body and close my eyes. I want this feeling of
> being enfolded, the relief of this turning away. Not
> a real affair—not the faked-out wife or late night
> rendezvous at Huddle House—just this. A hand strok-
> ing the back of my head, a still and quiet place apart
> from the pace of the world.

I look in the mirror once more to smooth down my hair against the late August humidity.

It isn't any particular person I want to lie down with and make my own. It isn't anybody at all. It is the feeling of being taken care of that I want to pin down and rock my hips against. Sling a leg across it and fall asleep.

This longing for body comfort and security is familiar as my own face.

The need is urgent.

THE NEED MAKES ME STUPID.

I dream about having an affair and for the first time I see through the dream to the longings beneath it. I feel SMART. I load my briefcase with books and papers and skip down the stairs to my car. I head for campus where I will lecture college students about literary motifs like FALLEN WOMEN and SALVATION and SACRIFICE and SCAPEGOATS, still thinking about my dream and the affair I might have and the mirror I looked into. I stand in front of the class with false courage, thinking SMART means SAFE. *If not love then surely knowledge can save me.* I break a sweat filling the board with notes, not yet grasping the difference between knowing and understanding.

Each word marks a gap in my psyche.

Internalization is not signaled by words but by silence when neurotic speech stops circling the gap.

EMILY AND I are sitting in her living room, the least well-heated room of the house, and my hands are cold. I tuck them between my knees.

Emily says, "You're not in touch with any of your exes?"

I say no and feel vaguely ashamed. Like she's giving me a psychological test. And I'm failing. I refill my wine glass and try to explain.

LESS THAN ONE year later, Emily and I are ensnared in an all-consuming affair with each other—flying in the face of her monogamous relationship of twelve years with a woman named Vanessa, risking our relationship as co-workers and friends—and the affair capsizes on the rocks and shoals of our separate needs.

I NEED TO TALK TO HER.
MY LIFE DEPENDS ON IT.
SHE TELLS ME THAT WON'T BE POSSIBLE.

"I need space," she says. She means for her monotone to defuse the conversation. I respond to the flat line of her voice by turning up the volume on my end—as if this contest of need requires a specific number of decibels and I have to make up for her deficit by making my own emotions louder—letting rip with a primal scream.

"YOU WANT SPACE?

YOU WANT SPACE?!

YOU'VE GOT IT."

I throw my phone at the wall. I cry. Scream again. Shake. I slam a kitchen cabinet door shut twenty times in a row. I clutch myself hard enough to leave bruises and drag my fingernails down the backs of my arms. I sit on the brand new Berber carpet in a room I keep neat as a pin and carve Emily's initials into my ankle, angled lines making rough letters like a child might draw. I think to myself, I NEVER WANT TO SEE HER AGAIN, clutching my foot and watching the letters bead up with blood.

THE NEXT DAY my face is swollen from crying. I keep getting pieces of cheap tissue stuck in my eyelashes. My hour of emergency psychotherapy is almost up.

"This is good," my therapist Paula tells me. "It's good this is happening to you. You tend to intellectualize. You need to feel this." We are two minutes past the hour. I write a check for the twenty-five dollar co-pay.

"I DON'T FEEL GOOD," I tell her.

"It will get better," she promises. "You won't always feel this way." I smile, nod, and stand to leave, but secretly I don't believe her.

THE "STRANGE SITUATION" WAS THE LABEL ASSIGNED IN 1969
TO A STANDARDIZED LABORATORY PROCEDURE IN WHICH
SEVERAL EPISODES, IN FIXED ORDER, WERE INTENDED TO
ACTIVATE AND/OR INTENSIFY INFANTS' ATTACHMENT BEHAVIOR.
THE ADJECTIVE "STRANGE" DENOTES "UNFAMILIAR," RATHER
THAN "ODD" OR "PECULIAR." IT WAS USED BECAUSE FEAR OF THE
UNFAMILIAR IS COMMONLY REFERRED TO AS "FEAR OF THE STRANGE."
—MARY D. SALTER AINSWORTH, E. WATERS, S. WALL,
Patterns of Attachment: A Psychological Study of the Strange Situation

IN THE 1960S a wave of scholarly attention rose up in the United States around the psychology of intimate attachment bonds, cresting in an experiment called the STRANGE SITUATION. The child developmental psychologists who devised the Strange Situation methodically activated attachment behaviors in their infant subjects—behaviors like seeking proximity to the caregiver, vocalizing distress, and demonstrating receptivity to feeding and holding—by having a mother leave her child briefly in an unfamiliar room where a stranger interacted with the child. The mother returned and engaged the infant. Then the psychologists recorded the reactions of infant to mother, generating a taxonomy of attachment styles—SECURE, AVOIDANT, AMBIVALENT, and (later) DISORGANIZED—to describe a child's sense of whether the object of her affection can be trusted to give comfort. The longer and more frequent the separations, the louder the protest cries and the longer the recovery time. Subsequent studies showed that sustained periods of separation—due to a mother's illness, a child's hospitalization, a parent's incarceration or death resulting in adoption, or the chronic emotional absence of depressed or drug addicted caregivers—create more serious rifts, sabotaging a child's core sense of security and sometimes turning a secure child avoidant or ambivalent.

By the late 1980s the American public sat transfixed by questions of love, sex, friendship, and intimacy. It was the era of *When Harry Met Sally,* and more urgent than the question of whether men and women can be friends was the question of whether adults can find comfort in each other or if disappointment, deceit, and sudden departures were to be expected instead. The nuclear family was all poltergeist and regret. As couples opted for no-fault divorces and kids faced the challenges of parents grieving separations and forming blended families, people wanted to understand the puzzle of romance. Social psychologists continued to work on the problem of intimacy, developing love quizzes and attachment interviews to measure the persistence of beliefs about self and other, from early pair-bonding between child and parent to adult romantic relationships.

Fatal Attraction, the second highest grossing film of 1987, dramatized American fears of *attachment gone awry.* In it, a woman named Alex Forrest (Glen Close) seduces and becomes obsessed with a man named Dan Callagher (Michael Douglas) to the point of stalking him, his wife, his daughter, and their ill-fated pet bunny. Despite the apparent presence of mental illness in this woman—who fakes a pregnancy, cuts her leg with a butcher knife, slits her wrists, and dissociates in the strobe light of her dark living room as she switches a table lamp on and off and on and off—the audience is poised to cheer when Alex meets her violent end.

———————————▸

THE VERY SAME YEAR, 1987, saw the development of the HAZAN-SHAVER ADULT ATTACHMENT INTERVIEW, a device to measure and compare attachment styles among adults. Most people fall into one of three categories derived from Mary Ainsworth's *Strange Situation,* each represented by a cluster of statements about optimal psychological space.

SECURE

I find it relatively easy to get close to others and am comfortable depending on them. I don't often worry about being abandoned or about someone getting too close to me.

AVOIDANT

I am somewhat uncomfortable being close to others; I find it difficult to trust them completely, difficult to allow myself to depend on them. I am nervous when anyone gets too close, and my partners often want me to be more intimate than I feel comfortable being.

ANXIOUS/AMBIVALENT

I find that others are reluctant to get as close as I would

like. I often worry that my partner doesn't really love me
or won't want to stay with me. I want to get very close
to my partner, and this sometimes scares people away.

—CINDY HAZAN AND PHILLIP R. SHAVER,
"Romantic Love Conceptualized
as an Attachment Process"

Research institutions like SUNY Stony Brook and UC Davis
established Adult Attachment labs for longitudinal studies of the adult
children subjected to the STRANGE SITUATION test in the late 1960s and
early 1970s.

Some people move confidently through the world, expecting to
return to a secure base at the end of every day. Others manage the
risk of being disappointed by remaining aloof and abdicating intimacy altogether. In between secure and avoidant there sits a riddle
called ANXIOUS-AMBIVALENT ATTACHMENT. People with ambivalent or
anxious-fearful attachment styles long desperately for intimacy but
their world is peopled with failures. They ask adulterers for loyalty
and they ask liars for honesty. They hide their true feelings, forget
the hiding place, and rage when no one can find them. They sharpen
the edges of ingenuity against the abrasive whetstone of a withhold-
ing lover. Security is always elsewhere. Preoccupied by its pursuit,
they walk into strange rooms and fold their bodies in strange arms
to study their own strange faces in the reflection of a stranger's eyes.

YOU WOULDN'T THINK IT COULD GET WORSE BUT IT DOES.

When security and anxiety are elicited by the same attachment figure, an endless loop is initiated: fear and the need for reassurance are followed by rejection and the intensification of fear. Approach and avoidance mesh in the person's gestures; she moves towards the mother but averts her eyes or turns around and walks backwards toward her. As adults, members of this group have trouble regulating their own emotions. They wonder who on earth would want them. Why belong to a club that would have you as a member?

Science labels them DISORGANIZED.

Family members just call them DIFFICULT.

TENTATIVE APPROACHES, MOVING SWIFTLY AWAY IMMEDIATELY UPON OR JUST FOLLOWING APPROACH TO THE PARENT, AND TENSE, VIGILANT BODY POSTURES ARE MARKERS FOR THE [DISORGANIZED] CATEGORY. THE DISORGANIZED ATTACHMENT STYLE OFTEN INVOLVES THE START, FOLLOWED BY THE INHIBITION, OF AN ATTACHMENT SEQUENCE. IT CAN BE CAUSED BY A FRIGHTENING, HOSTILE, OR INSENSITIVE MOTHER OR BY THE MOTHER'S OWN UNRESOLVED FEELINGS OF TRAUMA AND LOSS. THE INFANT IS PRESENTED WITH AN IRRESOLVABLE PARADOX WHEREIN THE HAVEN OF SAFETY IS AT ONCE THE SOURCE OF THE ALARM.

—MARY MAIN AND ERIK HESSE,
"Parents' Unresolved Traumatic Experiences Are
Related to Infant Disorganized Attachment Style"

I ENTERED HIGH SCHOOL THE SAME YEAR GLENN CLOSE BOILED HER LOVER'S BUNNY IN *FATAL ATTRACTION*. I was fourteen and infatuated with a boy who played trombone in the marching band. I had spoken to him in passing maybe twice. I maybe wanted to lose my virginity to him. I made eyes at him until his girlfriend threatened to blacken one of them. At home I panted at the television screen as young lovers sexed each other in bathtubs and on trains, the VCR squeaking as I hit pause and rewind. On the way to my piano teacher's house I picked up amber pieces of broken beer bottles from the sidewalk to shred the palms of my hands. My mother and I were estranged, and I fantasized that my language arts teacher loved me as if I were her daughter.

My classmates had my number from go.

You're a nice girl. But a little weird.

I graduated high school, got engaged, and moved out of my father's house to get away from his new wife, a woman with a gift for the passive-aggressive alienation of affections. She openly stated her intention to enter his life as a wedge between him and his daughters. He married her anyway and carved out a little paradise behind the house where her son could dive and splash in a new pool. I went to college fifteen minutes away but was asked to leave my house key before I left. I still have trouble resisting bitter envy toward the freshmen moving in each year at the university where I work, when I see their parents toting large plastic bags up the stairs bearing dorm decor from Target.

THE FEELINGS THAT struck me as enormous and unmanageable could have been easier to face and process had I seen them situated in simple conceptual maps like the two-dimensional model of interpersonal style published by Kim Bartholomew and Leonard Horowitz in the *Journal of Personality and Social Psychology* in August of 1991 as my second quarter of college began. It was out there but I had no access to it. One axis measures thoughts about self and another measures thoughts about other people, producing four basic categories of attachment.

	THOUGHTS ABOUT SELF	
	POSITIVE	NEGATIVE
POSITIVE	**Secure Attachment** Higher self-esteem Higher sociability	**Anxious Attachment** Lower self-esteem Higher sociability
THOUGHTS ABOUT OTHERS		
NEGATIVE	**Dismissive Attachment** Higher self-esteem Lower sociability	**Fearful Attachment** Lower self-esteem Lower sociability

Maybe I would not have gone crazy for the next fifteen years if ideas produced in ivory towers found their way more steadily and with less anti-intellectual distortion into the mainstream.

The field of adult attachment studies tempts the arm towards the blunt force of blame—*I'm fucked up and it's all your fault!*—but blaming external sources is not really the point of psychoanalytic theory. Instead of good parents and bad parents, theorists speak of more ambiguous things like the GOOD-ENOUGH MOTHER and the problem of the POOR FIT between child and environment. In nonoptimal parent-child relationships, the predictor of the adult child's approach to romance is not the parent's behavior but the ideas that form and clot in a child's mind to explain parent, self, other, and world with the uncanny logic of dreams and dark tales.

MY FATHER WAS a senior in high school in 1969—the same year Mary Ainsworth first published her findings from the Strange Situation experiment—and he still lived in his familiar home with his familiar parents and wanted to please them with his familiar life.

In two years he will smoke a MAGIC CIGARETTE with a STRANGE GIRL in a red miniskirt and fall instantly in love. She will lie and cheat and steal and sleep all day and at first he will think this is GRAND. She is so different from his family. He is mesmerized by this difference and makes a theater out of it, staging a drama of a world where day is night and night is day and people don't always choose work over play. She will liberate him from the demanding morals of his Puritan parents and he will stand close by her side like a proper disciple. She will teach him the freedom of not caring about other people when they say things like, *You hurt my feelings.*

One day she will come to him and say she is with child. She will say she doesn't know if it's his. She will say he has to marry her anyway.

She is testing him.

HE FAILS THE TEST.
He marries her.

Seven months later he smiles into my newborn face and invites me to become his accomplice in a heist of a very grand scale.

He asks if I can keep a secret.

I say yes.

The secret comes to me not in whispers but in sighs and innuendo. We are going to steal the red miniskirt fire from my mother. Then we are going to run away. After we leave we will cover our tracks by lying to everyone we meet.

"FIRE?" we'll exclaim like offended women. "We don't even like fire." We will say: *my mother is fire / fire is bad / we prefer ice / it's so tidy.*

We organize our faces into folded envelopes, like our new cool blue life is all we've ever known. Beneath the frozen ground, I bury wild memories of fire in an unmarked field and forget to mourn its loss.

My father teaches me THE TORMENT OF WANTING TO BURN.

Of hating what you want. Of wanting what you do not have. My father teaches me the shame of hiding my capacity for vice like a felony or a used syringe.

AFTER MY MOTHER he marries twice more. The second wife gives birth to a new self in nine months, her crazy breaking like water on the front steps of our house as she runs out the door. The third wife sets up an obstacle course in their home marked with signs in a language my father does not speak. He runs in circles and forgets to leave a bread-crumb trail for his daughters. We call his name in the woods but all we hear in response are echoes of our own voices.

I grow up thinking he got a raw deal. I grow up believing impatience made him reckless. I am impatient too. I leap without looking. My relationships are long hikes with irritating companions where I practice the art of the nonverbal complaint.

I reenact my father's story. . . .

THE DRAMA OF HAVING PICKED THE WRONG PERSON.

THE GENRE IS PSYCHOLOGICAL HORROR, shot in stark black and white. The heroine moves through her house in a phobic haze of self-doubt. Lights flicker and dim above her head. Pictures go missing from the walls. Footsteps echo from empty rooms.

Things are not what they seem.

The one who says I LOVE YOU is poised to deliver the most CUTTING BETRAYALS. Intimacy reveals itself as ruse. Frightened and mistrustful, I forgo my father's example and save myself from his fate in the forest of disenchantment. I flip the script. I do the opposite. I only know one way to make my life better.

GET ON THE BUS, GUS.

MAKE LIKE A TREE AND LEAVE.

I OPEN A bottle of wine with a picture of a monkey on it.

I am sitting on the balcony of my tiny new apartment watching the sky flush coral. One bedroom. Plain white walls. Bland beige carpet. Clean slate.

I am starting over again.

For more than ten months I listened every night to Anthony's paranoid fears of not being taken seriously at work and gave him advice and support when I could, but most of the time I just gave him the cold shoulder because secretly I despised him.

When I began to fantasize about killing him—a single blow to the head with a concrete block—I made his voice stop by moving out. Now I can relax.

I am putting things behind me.

> My mother's face when I left her house a day early
> because she was so high her eyes rolled back in her
> head when I talked to her.

> Anthony's face when I asked him not to visit me at my new
> apartment. His face is a stone surface worn smooth at
> the base of a waterfall. He is shocked and mystified by
> the fact that I want nothing to do with him now.

> My face when I buried it in my hands and cowered on
> the living room floor while Anthony screamed at me
> for describing him to a friend as a dark person.

Free as a bird, I fly from South Carolina to JFK to give a lecture at Barnard on feminist media studies and quality television. I dine with two Manhattan ladies who pay $12 for a glass of wine without blinking. One of the ladies is named Lila. I find myself in a fast crush on her. She wears a delicate necklace with a tiny o in silver that falls to the ocean bottom of her clavicle. I look at the o like a mouth open in surprise and think about kissing her. I tell her over dinner that I developed stage fright out of the blue this fall. In a gesture of intimacy on par with a kiss she hands me a pill. She feeds me fragments of it. One at dessert. One she brings to me at the stage where I am preparing to speak. I love Lila a little bit. I go home and tell Emily. She is my coworker and I solaced myself with benign romantic thoughts of her during my unhappy cohabitation with Anthony.

I WANT SOMETHING FROM EMILY BUT I DON'T KNOW WHAT.

A member of the English department dies unexpectedly. The rest of us pass his office door with our mouths closed in mourning.

I picture the mass of lung cancer hiding behind his sternum since last spring.

I picture Emily and me lying side by side on my bed and holding hands.

I GO TO the ocean with Emily and two other friends where we drink wine under a full moon to remind ourselves that being alive can be beautiful. I go to Thanksgiving dinner at her house and talk her ear off in the kitchen. I wish we could eat our plates of turkey and cranberry sauce over the sink while everyone else makes small talk in another room. The New Year comes and I go to Emily's house to watch television. She introduces me to the genre of dyke drama. We eat rich artichoke dip and drink big glasses of red wine. We pause the show and I ask personal questions like when she first knew she was a lesbian, how it started, if she ever had boyfriends. She tells me her history. I'm curious because I wonder if I might be a lesbian too.

I lean towards her when she admits past infidelities.

"So," I say. "You're a CHEATER," lining the word with wool like a wolf. "Tell me more," I say. "Tell me everything."

Her throat opens like a morning glory.

I reciprocate by telling stories about my mother. When I express the profound loneliness I experienced as a child, Emily listens and tilts her head just right.

SOMETHING UNFURLS IN ME.

I tell her my mother showed me the shape the clock hands would make when it was time to walk down to the road to catch a yellow school bus winding through the mountains into Maggie Valley where I lived. I tell her I stood at the end of the driveway in the cold and concentrated on willing the bus to appear. I tell her I came home hungry at the end of the school day and held my aching head in my hands while my mother ran errands.

I tell her I ran into our unfinished basement crying because my mother didn't love me and called my best friend Penny Moss to confess. I needed someone else to know.

I wanted Penny Moss to make me feel better. It was like asking a brand new acquaintance to drive me to the airport or feed my cat when I leave town. Forced. Premature. Out of place.

We were maybe only best friends in my head.

Penny Moss and I were not friends at all by the next week. We warred for popularity on the playground. Penny marched in one direction with a group of girls behind her. I marched in the other direction with others girls lined up in lockstep behind me.

We face off. All the girls circle round.

Penny pulls out her trump card. She points at me and shouts,

"HER MOTHER DOESN'T EVEN LOVE HER."

I hold my breath and wait. I feel the anonymous pinches of small girl fingers, the twist and burn of girl hands on my forearms, the yank and sting of pulled hair. I see the spots bald of rabbit fur on my new winter coat. But the whirling girl dervish I anticipate never descends. Instead they turn on Penny in anger.

"No one's mother doesn't love them."

They walk away in twos and threes. Being unloved by my mother is unthinkable. They can't imagine it.

I walk away too.

FOR YEARS I will repeat the secret that my mother doesn't love me to friends and family, lovers and strangers, over and over to take the sting out of it.

"You tell everyone everything," Emily says. "The first night I met you, you told me you were having an affair with a married man, you were bisexual, and you were in terrible debt but digging your way out. It's refreshing actually, the way you pour your heart out. But I wonder if that moment on the playground is the reason why. I wonder if it all goes back to Penny Moss." Emily pauses and takes a sip of wine, still thinking about Penny betraying me on the playground. "I can't believe she did that. That BITCH." I top off her glass and smile wider.

I tell Emily about the morning I noticed two bumps on the back of my head—one on the left side and one on the right—near the base of my skull. My mother is equal parts hysteric and hypochondriac and she instilled in me an expectation of sudden catastrophe. Our bodies might sprout a fairy circle of tumors. Our bodies made us shiver in fear and disgust. We looked in the mirror and prepared ourselves to be horrified.

I watched my mother stick long Q-tips inside her caesarian sutures to clean the wound when it wept and bled and split open. I walked into the kitchen one day and saw two bags hanging over the stove dripping purple liquid into a large pan. I worried her body had rejected her new silicone breast implants. I worried she had to remove them. But it was just grapes from our yard. She was making jelly. I saw a peach pit on the edge of the bathroom sink and recalled my mother digging under the skin of her face with a needle that morning. I worried she had pulled some piece of gore from her body. When I feel the two bumps on the back of my head, I think my body is revolting too.

I show them to my mother and ask what they are.

"Horns. You're growing goat horns."

I think about our goat Toro's horns before they grew from his head—little nubs, hard beneath the surface of his skin. Just like mine.

"Better watch out," she deadpans. *"They'll show through your hair soon."*

Five years pass before I realize she was lying.

I wait five years to be revealed as part goat, part girl.

I tell Emily I ran away from home when I was eleven. I packed my books and T-shirts in paper sacks and hid them beneath the low-hanging branches of a magnolia tree at the far edge of the yard. My father would pick me up that Friday afternoon and maybe never bring me back. I tell her I ran through the yard with my arms full and held my breath as I opened the door to come back inside. If Mother caught me she would string me up in the yard and carve TRAITOR on my forehead.

I helped take care of my youngest sister Melissa for the first two years of her life, bathing and feeding her and sometimes getting up in the middle of the night to quiet her from crying. I thought about getting married in four years when I turned fifteen and adopting Melissa so she could grow up without being called bad names.

BRATS. DUMBASSES. BITCHES. SLUTS.
Our friends were IDIOTS and WHORES.

Emily and I cover our mouths in horror as we laugh. "I don't know why I'm laughing," she says. "It's so awful I can hardly stand it."

"It is horrible, isn't it?" I like that she doesn't dismiss me with a wry toast to Freud or Nancy Friday.

"I can just picture you," she tells me. "Standing alone at the end of your driveway, waiting for the bus. You're so brave. That's who you are. That brave little girl."

Emily misunderstands me from the very beginning but I won't let myself know this for a very long time.

I CAN'T. I NEED TO BELIEVE I HAVE FOUND THE ONE.

Emily would say I underestimate her. She cared more for me than I realize and understood me better than I think. I will become so confused by her I won't even recognize the truth when she offers it to me. *"My name is Emily!"* she will say to me and I will scream in her face to stop lying.

I drain my wine glass and stare at the black windowpane behind me, my mind suddenly empty. I can't tell if Emily might love me or if she might just be looking at me through a glass case in a museum of deformed curiosities.

Goat girl. Monster.

Soon everyone will know.

I walked around my house as a young girl with my shoulders hunched. I flinched a lot. I took my mother's words hard. I believed she despised me. I believed I was despicable.

Some days even now I want to close the blinds and hide. I drive home from Emily's house feeling ashamed. I said too much. I stayed too late.

Imago. Ghost partner. Parent image. The unconscious wants to become whole. It wants to heal the wounds of childhood. In its pocket lies a detailed picture of the proper match. The one who will cover the shortfalls of childhood and fill the psychological gaps left by imperfect caretakers. How do we return to these gaps? By falling madly in love with someone who has both the positive and the negative traits of our imperfect parents, someone who fits an image that we carry deep inside us and for whose embodiment we are unconsciously searching.

When I fell into the blankness of Emily's dark windowpane, what did I not want to see? What did I not want to know?

I disliked her as much as I liked her.

She made me uncomfortable. The discomfort was familiar.

Emily probed the open sockets in my mouth with her tongue while her fingers wandered mindlessly over rough edges of old scabs, lifting them up before new layers grew strong and pink. She dabbed blood from my knee with a cloth napkin dipped in wine and smiled wider when I winced. I left her house hurting. I tossed left and right, then right and left, through the restless dreamless night.

"You must have had a terrible relationship with your mother," said the wife of the last married man I dated. Two years before the affair with Emily I sat across a bistro table in Barnes & Noble with a woman training to become a therapist. We were discussing her husband. She wanted me to understand that our attachment was a symptom of his unresolved conflicts with his parents and my unresolved conflicts with mine.

How dare she? I thought. *What malarkey.* Her words insulted me.

The sensation of insult masked an important fact.

What she said about the affair was true.

My illicit obsessive fixation on her husband was a vehicle for revisiting the mysteries and emotions of my childhood, but I wasn't developmentally mature enough yet to read the road signs or to recognize where I was going.

My mother and I are the original romantic couple.

She brings a criminal thrill to the mundane and I eagerly accept the invitation to an outlaw apprenticeship at her knee. We are late for things. We are not where we say we are. We sleep in and skip school / skip basketball practice / skip ballet. We read trashy novels thick with women gasping and being carried away by their passions.

On the way to the grocery store she tells me to watch for the fuzz while she smokes one of the joints we rolled together this morning. Our fingers worked together to sort seeds from the shake as if Mary-Jane were maize and we were two Cherokee princesses preparing for the Green Corn festival. I want to be let into her secret society so I boldly ate the seeds. I want her wildness to grow inside me. I want her to like me as much as I like her. I want her to recognize herself in me.

She says we are ON THE LAM. She says we are LOW RIDING.

I slouch deeper in the backseat and sing along with Rod Stewart on the radio. *If you think I'm sexy and you want my body, come on baby let me know.*

I am seducing my mother. I want her to want me.

I know I was a mistake. I know I don't belong.

My mother throws shade like a legendary drag queen. She brings out secrets with the sharp surprise of a blade beneath the tongue.

YOUR SISTER IS MY FAVORITE.
HE DOESN'T WANT YOU—
HE'S NOT EVEN YOUR REAL FATHER.

She points at my body and laughs at my modesty and tells my father when I grow pubic hair. She mocks me for thinking I have something to hide. I play straight man to her comedy routine like a breeder at the queer cabaret.

Do not try to pass as well adjusted in this place, the queen warns. *Show us your banji realness before we scratch off that mask you call a face.* If I am too loud or too slow or too needy she tells me to cram it and get lost.

Go play in the street. Take a long walk off a short pier.

I step out of her limelight and too-hot-ness and retreat to another room where I rock my baby sister to sleep—two losers clutching each other in the dark and calling it a hug. My red face and tangled hair tell the truth about this moment. I cry like rejection hurts but really I'm seething and planning to leave.

At eleven I'm already more criminal than martyr.

The image of one sister comforting another is a trick backlit and cropped tight. In the shadows outside the frame, a rubber mallet and several large garbage bags sit neatly by my feet.

LIGHT AS A FEATHER STIFF AS A BOARD. I lie still enough to disappear. I say CANDYMAN CANDYMAN CANDYMAN. I'd rather be anywhere other than here. I choose the company of demons over my drag of a mother. She confuses meanness with having a ball. She reads me but doesn't get me at all.

"WHY ARE YOU considering visiting your mother this summer?" my therapist asks, more than twenty years later. For years people have been asking me some version of this question. I haven't seen my mother in five years and I often think of a weekend reunion in Georgia, but every time I visit the story is always the same. We have fun for a while. Then we argue and I run away crying.

My therapist suggests placing limits on our time together. Maybe I could meet her for lunch instead of staying at her house. I scan the molding along the edge of the ceiling and reflect on why this would be the worst solution ever.

If I'm going to see my mother, then I need to see her at home. I need to see her in bed. Like royalty, she takes visitors from atop her king size bed. The inner circle may join her there. We serve at her pleasure. We are dismissed at her bidding. We sit on top of the comforter with pillows stacked behind us like we get bruises from tiny peas. We watch avidly as soap divas wax histrionic at the touch of a magical button. As afternoon turns to evening, the jesters in the box play Jersey Mafiosi and serve cold dishes of revenge. Our errands are done and we retreat from the irritations of dry cleaning and mall traffic in the perfect bliss of caffeine and codeine and companion animals that adore us. Her Maltese wrestles with my Shih Tzu and they yip with glee at our return. My mother wonders aloud what the dogs are saying as if they spoke Swedish or Urdu.

I hesitate at the idea of meeting for lunch because I don't want to put our bipolar relationship on mood stabilizers. I fear some kind of loss, our mother-daughter bond dull as old silver.

I like being ADDICT and BEDMATE and OUTLAW.
Favorite daughter. Fairest of all.

The first time I developed a crush on someone else's boyfriend I was nine.

I spent my teenage years riding back roads with boys who did not belong to me drinking Two Fingers Tequila from the bottle. I seek partners who belong to other people and then work mightily at convincing them to meet my needs.

Choose me.

I have affairs. I thieve love. I beg for it.

PEOPLE WANT WHAT THEY CANNOT HAVE.

I see people in relationships as compromised by definition. Delusional. I am their rude awakening. I sleep with their husbands and wives like snapping my fingers in front of their faces to break the romantic trance. I steal their social security and call it a free service for the legally blind and cognitively impaired.

I help them understand how the story ends.

BOOM I got your boyfriend.
HA HA I got your man.

I sing along with MC Luscious in a full-body euphoric flush, never wondering why the love triangle holds such irresistible appeal for me. Even after white-knuckling a seven month loop-de-loop on Emily's Romantic Mindbender, a rickety runaway train, I will enter therapy with my defenses up, and when the issue of my attachment patterns comes up, I will swat at the obviousness of the observation, waving it like a pest from the wet places on my face.

RUBYFRUIT MASOCHIST

DAPHNE LONEY GETS ME.

She lives in New Orleans and she doesn't know me but she totally gets me. She makes sculptures about the psychology of personal space. Her titles clap and stomp to the awkward beat of my hot-coal dance around boundaries.

DEVICE THAT ATTRACTIVELY PREVENTS PHYSICAL CONTACT FROM STRANGERS, FRIENDS, AND FAMILY. DEVICE THAT PREVENTS ANYONE FROM COMPULSIVELY HUGGING YOU. APPARATUS THAT ENABLES ONE TO GIVE THE ILLUSION OF CONFIDENCE WHILE CAUSING YOURSELF DIS-COMFORT. They are metal collars. Wire. Copper. Glass.

I tape a picture of one of these sculptures on my office door as a way of warning my colleagues and supervisors and students in advance. I am hard to get close to. I put this fact on blast as if it's something to be proud of. As if it's funny.

Large spent bullet shells jut out from the neck.
A magnifying glass curves upwards towards the face
of the woman wearing the collar. One collar extends
down the chest with a plate of metal bearing two-foot
long extensions ending in a thick protruding nail.

Everything about me sends the same message. Intimacy hurts.
I dare you to kiss me anyway.

I INVITE EMILY to my place and all the surfaces glitter. The table is covered in crystal candlestick holders and stemmed glassware for three different kinds of alcohol. I have created a glistening surface for my life as a defense against chronic depression. Emily calls the condo my bachelorette pad. She sees the life of the single girl as one long afternoon without obligations, but I've been single most of my adult life and I miss the sensation of belonging with someone. The condo is less MEDITATION RETREAT than REFUGEE CAMP or TRIAGE STATION.

I fear Emily sees me as defective *you're not in touch with any of your exes? you tell everyone everything! that bitch Penny Moss turned you into a goat* so I drench the atmosphere in the erotic. I do this. Turn critics into lovers. Afterwards, when we still don't get along, I am mystified by my failed attempt to neutralize conflict by merging with its source.

Emily had flirted with me in an email message *you looked fabulous in your green scarf* and I want to appear open and unfazed. I come to the door in a low-cut satin tank top lined with black lace. I compliment her thin silk sweater *très chic! c'est chouette!* and embrace her like we are Parisian. I delay the kiss with Emily so long she says, "This is silly. I'm going home." After hours of strained flirtation I press my closed lips to her closed lips and wait to see what happens.

THE MATCH IGNITES.

THE UNCONSCIOUS FALLS IN LOVE.

THE CHANCE OF A POSITIVE OUTCOME IS SLIM INDEED.

THE KISS IS NOT MAGICAL.
THE KISS IS CHEMICAL.

The life we knew before no longer exists. We have abandoned the present and joined hands as traveling companions in a novel of seduction set in the distant past.

We read the book like the pages are on fire.

WHEN I WAS a teenager in rural Georgia I never thought I'd get the chance to kiss a girl.

I fantasized about it as early as fifteen after stumbling across a classic lesbian coming-of-age novel called *Rubyfruit Jungle* in a local bookstore, but I couldn't imagine how it would ever happen. No one in my high school was out. The only lesbian I knew was old and unattractive. I had private crushes on girls and channeled the sexual energy into my boyfriend.

The year after my divorce I didn't want to sleep alone at night and didn't care whose body curled behind mine as I drifted off, so I opened myself to new sexual possibilities.

That spring I date a married couple about eight years older than me. We go from a bar to my rented house and listen to music in my bedroom. The three of us sit in a row on the edge of my bed like school children. Tad, the husband, sits in the middle. He tells me to kiss his wife. I can't imagine what will happen when our lips touch. I have been raised to believe our parts won't fit. I picture a Plexiglas window popping up between us. Soon I am more interested in Julia than her husband even though he was the one who initially attracted me. I love kissing Julia and I hate lying in bed with Tad while she showers for work. I am uncomfortable and I can't tell how much of the weirdness is from the threesome dynamics and how much is from the girl-girl sex. The two feelings converge and crash over my head so hard I stop taking their calls.

When I see them in a record store the following spring, I WALK THE OTHER WAY.

Over the next decade I will have a string of one-night stands with women to remind myself I'm attracted to women and to prove I'm not afraid of this attraction.

THE TRUTH IS
THE ATTRACTION SCARES ME A LOT.

"I think you're a lesbian," my younger sister Jessica tells me one day when I'm in my mid-twenties. She came out in high school after I asked her advice about whether I should tell my boyfriend that I kissed my friend Kate. Her first reaction was panic. She started sobbing and hung up on me, but soon she admitted she was gay and shot past me in achieving the markers of lesbian legitimacy—dating women, developing a circle of friends who two-step at lesbian bars, meeting the love of her life on Myspace and moving to Massachusetts to marry her—while I kept sex with girls safely outside my sense of real life.

"I'm not a lesbian," I tell her.

I confine LESBIAN to the blur of late night margins. I insist LESBIAN is all lark and dare for me.

I am in love with a man named Jack when we have this conversation—a man who cooks for me, slices oranges for me, drinks whiskey from a bottle in the tub with me, pins me to the wall of his bedroom by my wrists and pounds his body into mine until I scream from the intensity—and the awkward nights in bed with my stripper friends and graduate school girlfriends pale in comparison.

"Don't you think that's because you keep making out with straight women?" asks Jessica.

The question gives me pause but mostly I still feel like an imposter. I don't know what lesbians do in bed. I don't want to be revealed as remedial. My sister told me to draw the alphabet with my tongue between Emily's legs, but the plan does not leave me relaxed or confident.

I am still unsure of my sexual orientation and I fear my lesbian lark may end in social exile.

"I need to renew my bisexual street cred," I joke to my sister, even though my real feelings are not this breezy or superficial. I don't want to overstate my claim to same-sex desire at this time for at least three separate reasons.

- *I don't want to look like a poser.*
- *I don't want to find myself in over my head.*
- *And I don't want to be rejected.*

I can no more imagine Emily wanting me than my lady professor of British Lit years ago, the one who hosted cookouts at her house for English majors each spring. I stayed late into the night talking books and grad school on her patio, prolonging my access to her home life and leisure hours. In class I studied the poem of her face while she lectured on the literary meanings of fruitwet woman bodies and said things like *brothels are built with the bricks of religion and prisons with the stones of law.* THAT'S HOT. I had a crush on her *and* her husband. My feelings fell in the overlapping spaces between wanting to be them, wanting to sex them, and wanting to be claimed by them as their brilliant adopted daughter.

Emily is equally out of my league, always put together just so in slacks, silk blouses, and sharp-toed shoes brought to you by the letter V. She owns a house! She makes pasta salads! Emily is nine years older than I am. She has a partner. They have a daughter. I'm not a lesbian. The odds are against an affair. Yet here she is, her lips pressed against my lips, offering to stay the night.

I don't take her up on it.

I don't want to act on impulse.

I wait a week. I need to think through the pluses and minuses of an affair with Emily. Number one in the minus column is the fact that we're coworkers. I don't want to lose the comfort of campus. I like my office and my department. I don't want to let the infatuation and chaos of romance bleed into these clean spaces. Number one in the plus column is the fact of external controls. Emily is in a long-term relationship and her partner, Vanessa, is probably moving back to town in a few months, so we will have to end the affair after a short period of exploration and fun.

No hearts broken.

Just passing the time.

Before the first kiss, though, she asks if I'm flirting because I'm bored and I say no. I say I'd be interested even if we lived somewhere with lots of lesbians.

Both perceptions are true. I am interested in her. I am glad the external controls will end the relationship. This structure feels safe. The stakes are low. We won't have to consider the hard questions.

ARE WE COMPATIBLE? DO WE WANT TO DO THIS FOREVER?

Do you love me as much as I love you? Should we move in together?

Will you always use this *towel to wipe the counters in the kitchen and leave* this *towel on the oven door just for drying clean hands?*

We will not have to do algebraic equations of intimacy. Vanessa will come back to town and take her away from me. Problem solved. No reason to worry at evenly matching our levels of devotion.

I weave this logic into a security blanket.

Pull it snugly up to my chin.

After the first sexual encounter with Emily I feel a panic attack coming on but I mask it so as not to be impolite. I get up to take some sinus medication. I peel back the metal foil and swallow the pill but I still can't breathe. Something is in the way.

The fine print on the box should give a warning.

PSEUDOEPHEDRINE IS NOT FDA-APPROVED FOR ENGULFMENT FEARS.

I am already thinking about how to extract myself from the situation. Emily asks if she should leave and I say no. I smile reassuringly at her and we snuggle together like peas in a pod. I fumble with invisible straps and buttons and pull on a large imaginary metal collar so she won't flow over my head and pull me out to sea. I close my mouth around a tube and pull air through a too-narrow passageway, my untrained lungs aching from the pressure.

Laura Tuley calls Daphne Loney's metalcollar
sculptures "three-dimensional representations
of the psychological prisons women erect for
themselves in order to perform and function by
the prevailing norms of feminine etiquette, and
the ways women defend themselves from the toxic
effects of these norms."

WHAT HAVE I GOTTEN MYSELF INTO?

I'm afraid she's going to fall in love with me. I'm afraid she's going to want me more than I want her. I'm afraid I'll turn cold and stop talking to her and not be able to explain why. Emily draws circles on my back with her fingertips until I feel calm but I never do go to sleep that night. Before she leaves the next morning we make plans to see each other the following weekend. And as I begin to breathe again in the birdsong of daybreak part of me can't wait.

The show is not about the oppression but about the
participation of women in their own confinement.
On a socio-political level, the work evokes the white
lies women resort to in order to deny others access
to them or otherwise protect themselves from the
social obligations that frame their lives.

MY SISTER WAS RIGHT. Sex with a lesbian is better than sex with straight girls. It is also better (for me) than sex with men. In bed with Emily my body becomes a field of delight instead of the problem men marked it—Woody Allens, all of them, complaining in unison about sore jaws—and I never leave the bed anymore without reaching orgasm. The climax becomes one point in a wide circle of erotic energy that passes from my body to hers and from hers back to mine, and I learn what straight girls everywhere need to learn. Getting a girl off isn't that difficult. And if his jaw hurts from how long it takes for you to get there, he's doing it wrong. OR POSSIBLY YOU ARE GAY.

More than one boyfriend has recommended I seek medical treatment for not getting wet like his other girlfriends, but I no longer fall short in that area. I almost come from pushing my body towards her body and listening to the sounds she makes in response. I hold her down and press her body into the couch, moving my hips against her until she gasps and closes her eyes.

I am exploring the subtle power dynamics of being a FEMME TOP. I run the fuck.

I practice LESBIAN like an intricate piece of sheet music for advanced piano. I become aware of LESBIAN as something beyond orientation. LESBIAN unfolds in me as ontology, epistemology, phenomenology, and sexology. I stand in the South Carolina landscape with a wider stance. I cut my fingernails short and walk with deliberate strides. I play and laugh and roll around with her on the floor.

Emily and I abandon our real lives and glide across the water of our lives as if the affair is a gondola and the world is our theme park. We are silly and self-indulgent. We buy lacey panties and T-shirts with ironic statements across the chest.

Mine says, TRUST ME.
Hers says, I DON'T GIVE A HOOT!

We buy gemstone earrings and get third holes pierced in our ears. Emily makes me promise I will never take it out.

"I won't go if you don't promise."

So I promise. She puts one pink stud in her ear and I put one pink stud in mine. We behave like eighth-graders exchanging BFF heart necklaces for Christmas.

One broken half on one necklace. One broken half on the other.

WHEN WE HAVE SEX I think about Emily's partner.

Vanessa standing at the open door of Emily's bedroom while we swirl and moan. Vanessa pulling into the driveway and catching us in the act. Vanessa being forced to watch. Vanessa hurting. I stare at a sepia-toned picture of Emily and Vanessa in a frame above the nightstand and my pelvis rocks faster at the thought of trespass, my pleasure a five-fingered discount.

When I leave Emily's house to rush to a meeting after a noonday tryst in front of her closet mirror, I am so high on endorphins I can hardly drive. My fingertips buzz with pleasure. It coats me like suntan oil.

The pinks of the blooming crepe myrtles are pinker than ever before. I want to roll around in the petals piled beneath them. I want to scoop them up in handfuls and shower Emily with them.

A woman on the radio sings, I LOVE YOU I LOVE YOU I LOVE YOU I LOVE YOU. I turn the volume up and put my foot on the gas.

Pseudo-love.

If a person has not reached the level where she has a sense

of I-ness rooted in the productive unfolding of her own powers,

she tends to idolize the loved person. She is alienated from

her own powers and projects them into the loved person.

The bearer of all love, all light, all bliss.

In this process she deprives herself of all sense of strength,

loses herself in the loved one instead of finding herself. Since

no person can live up to the expectations of her idolatrous

worshiper, disappointment is bound to occur.

Emily recommends a film—*you'll love it,* she says, *I can't wait to hear what you think*—and in the cool dark plush of the theater I watch men and women fall in love with each other and cheat on each other and fall apart over each other like lesbians on television. I read it like a love note in code.

"Do you know what a heart looks like?" Clive Owen bellows at Jude Law.

"A fist wrapped in blood!"

The image is wonderful and gruesome and strange and I wonder what Emily is trying to tell me. Clive Owen looks sort of like our colleague Lyle. I personally think Lyle lingers in Emily's office too often. When I roam down the hallway at work and knock on her office door where I plan to flirt and moon, sometimes Lyle is already there. I think Lyle should fuck off. I retreat and email Emily.

Instead of telling her I'm jealous I tell her about managing my jealousy. I SEE THIS INDIRECTNESS AS SOPHISTICATION. *I rock the coy disguise like oversized D&Gs hiding peagreen eyes.*

Date: February 4, 2005
To: Emily
From: Lisa
Conversation: film review

Dear Emily—

I heard Jude Law say that *Closer* is about the fact that we only see about 50% of the person with whom we are in a relationship and the effort to force out the rest of a person's story/self/secrets is precisely what destroys the relationship. I will therefore refrain from forcing you to further reenact your conversation with Lyle. Instead I will simply say I look forward to our own outing next weekend. And to season two of *The L Word,* which is right around the corner.

xxoo—
L

This is jealousy intellectual-style!

Meta-jealousy.

A discourse on jealousy. Anything but jealousy itself.

Jealousy itself would be gauche. Jealousy is so yesterday. I want to be so TODAY I'm already TOMORROW. I want to be bigger than my jealousy. I want to be above it.

I know insecurity is unattractive. I hate this side of me.

I don't really hate this side of me.

I think other people will hate it so I hate it preemptively to ward off the unbearable feeling of having my shortcomings pointed out by other people. I want to get there before anyone else and stake my claim on hating my jealousy so no one else can.

Emily says jealousy is a perfectly normal feeling.

She lets me off the hook just like that.

> *The collars are made of metal. Handcuffs.*
>
> *Cement block. Hysterical symptom.*
>
> *Everyone is subject to neuroses. Some of us are*
>
> *able to disguise them or wear them more attractively.*

"Remember," she emails me, "I love EVERYTHING about you."

I want to rest easy in her reassurance but I won't let myself. I intend to outsmart the gamble of intimacy.

I put my money on FALSE every time.

HYSTERICAL PAROXYSM;
OR, THE CASE OF THE WANDERING UTERUS

IT IS VALENTINE'S DAY EVE and I finally send Emily the love note she's been asking for, having no idea the short message will hit us both like a truck. Before I hit send, I copy my sophomoric attempt at the erotic from work email to non-work email. What I don't know is this. Emily shares her AOL account with Vanessa. Worse, Vanessa already suspects something. The next morning, on a day when I plan to bring a box of truffles to my secret sweetheart, I get a panic-brief message from Emily with the subject line, "life imitating art, sort of."

The body of the email reads, "I need to talk to you."

I call Emily right away and she sounds distant and annoyed. She tells me Vanessa called at 7:00 AM. She tells me Vanessa knows. Her clipped rhythm is unfamiliar and hard to read. Is she angry? Is she in shock? I feel small and scared and embarrassed.

I sit paralyzed on the phone. All I can say is—

OH. MY. GOD.

I feel heat on my face as if I'm sitting in front of a fire. All I can think about is how to make this feeling go away. I invite Emily over to talk that evening and sweat minutes like bullets. The clock force-marches morning into the grim showdown of afternoon. When Emily arrives we sit together on my couch like women in a hospital waiting room. *Will she make it? How bad was the wreck? Has it been determined whether anyone was at fault? Do you know if she has insurance?* We repeat words like BLINDSIDED and JAWS OF LIFE. We are stunned. Nothing in this crazy world makes sense.

It is Valentine's Day and I am disoriented by romantic whiplash.

The normal guardrails of healthy emotional boundaries were never constructed inside me. I think it's normal that I feel what Emily feels. Better than normal: I believe tuning into other people's emotions is my secret superpower. I can bend steel with my bare hands. I can find a way in. I am CAPTAIN EMPATHY—able to intuit feelings like Superman leaps tall buildings. In a single bound. I see boundaries as limits. I don't want any. Robert Frost says good fences make good neighbors but every-one knows he secretly fantasizes about swinging from birches. The fence thing is just Frost being afraid of his own queer passions.

One could do worse than be a swinger of birches, you know?

Fences are for cowards.

I lied before. I do want her to tell me everything. I do want her to reenact the entire conversation.

I want more than 50 percent.

> LIKE A SPONGE, THE MATE WITH BOUNDARIES SET
> TOO CLOSE ABSORBS EVERY FROWN, EVERY
> TIGHTENED JAW, AND FEELS RESPONSIBLE FOR IT.
> —ANNE KATHERINE, *Boundaries: Where You End and I Begin*

I dump the contents of my heart in her lap and gesture for her to pony up. I wait for her to say something but her jaw is wired shut.

SCENARIO 1: Vanessa might break up with Emily and Emily might die of heartache and/or embarrassment. Vanessa might reveal our affair to the department chair. She might create scandal and spur reprimand. She might withdraw her hat from the ring in our search for a new faculty member. She is a top candidate. This could be bad for my career. I ask careful questions to gauge Emily's temperature. I watch her face for signs of fever. I want to know if the prospect of a breakup makes her sad (in which case she might hate me) or happy (in which case she might love me). This is a lot of pressure on an affair of barely three weeks.

SCENARIO 2: Vanessa might not break up with Emily and the death by heartache might be mine instead. Vanessa might take the job, reclaim her partner, and send me packing. This seemed like a comforting idea just a few days ago but now it starts to sting. What if Emily and I are meant for more than an affair? What if we should be together? Is it something she might want? Is it something I might want?

We don't know what will happen. We don't know how we feel.

I want to be like Maureen in a book I'm reading about boundaries. Her husband walks in and complains about everything he sees. MAUREEN STAYS CALM AND RINSES THE VEGETABLES. MAUREEN STAYS IN HER OWN PSYCHOLOGICAL SPACE.

"I don't know what caused this mood of yours,"
she says, "but I know I'm okay."
And then she leaves the room.

I am not Maureen. I know I'm not okay. I am nose to nose with a fire and it's too hot. I want to fix the fire—as if the fire itself were uncomfortable, as if the discomfort I feel were not my own.

I want to make the fire feel better. I want to love it to ashes.

WHEN THE SEARCH COMMITTEE selects Vanessa for the job two days later, I tell Emily to say whatever she has to say to get Vanessa to take the job. My anxiety about holding on to Emily is the scratchy heat of a wool sweater in early spring, uncomfortable but manageable. My anxiety about maintaining the department's approval is a feather pillow against my face. I have to get out from under it. Vanessa takes the job. Emily and I set a date to end the affair. Spring break.

"Like ripping off a Band-Aid!" I say.
The week comes and goes but we do not break up.

Getting caught mobilizes a dynamic of scarcity.
There might not be enough love to go around.

The idea that we can't be together drives us both crazy. We cling. We panic. We glut ourselves on each other. We synchronize our schedules. If Emily makes plans with someone else—lunch with a friend in the next town over, breakfast with a colleague at a local diner—I fume, *How could she?* We spend hours on the phone unable to say goodbye even when we are exhausted or have other things to do or have absolutely nothing left to say.

"I would gladly just listen to you breathe," as if this proves something. I long to hang up but refuse to give in. I am dedicated to this irrational race. I run towards the ribbon as if running were its own reward.

"You always seemed so—"

Emily reaches for a word and I lean into the empty space I have become inside her mouth, hoping to be flattered and made new—

"self-contained."

"Now that you know the truth about me," I ask, "are you horrified?"

My question is not a genuine invitation to intimacy. I use it to block the possibility of judgment. It is a request for REASSURANCE. It is a demand that she COLLUDE with my lies and CONFIRM my psychological alibis. We make a deal to dedicate ourselves to mutual emotional rescue and fall in love not with each other but with this deal. This false intimacy has a name in psychology.

It's called a NEUROTIC PACT.

We begin to admit enmeshment. Neither of us is sleeping or eating well. We are not resting or exercising. We are in a relationship. That is our whole job on this earth. We push risotto around on our plates, stab the occasional olive. We leave half-eaten meals on the table and fall into bed. We drink on empty stomachs and wake up with headaches. Our bodies shrink. I hold my breath and hope for hypnosis. I need to hear the words. *You win the prize. I will love you forever. You are worth losing everything else.* Jackpot. Home base. An umpire whispers in my ear, "You're safe."

I enter the affair thinking of it as a light and meaningless thing, a diversion, but when Emily does not leave me as she promises Vanessa she will our feelings balloon and sway. We say *I love you* like we mean it and this speech act changes everything. I feel entitled to more from her. Soon I am weeping on the phone in outrage at impermanence, disappointment, and loss. I weep at my own foolishness.

> WITH THE INFALLIBILITY OF A SLEEPWALKER,
> SHE SEEKS OUT THOSE WHO, LIKE HER PARENTS,
> CANNOT UNDERSTAND HER. SHE WILL TRY TO MAKE
> HERSELF UNDERSTANDABLE TO PRECISELY THESE PEOPLE.
> SHE WILL TRY TO MAKE POSSIBLE WHAT CANNOT BE.
> —ALICE MILLER, *Drama of the Gifted Child*

"How could I not have known? All this time?" I arrived late to the lesbian party. I don't want it to wind down so soon.

"Can I call you later to check on you?" she asks. "Would you mind?"

I scream into the phone like a child. "If you don't, I'll hate you for the rest of my life!" Tantrum voice. Three years old.

Emily says, "You're adorable." She doesn't realize something has been revealed. Something neither of us will find attractive in the months to come.

Be terribly crazy my darling. I will anticipate you.

I can hear the promise clear as a bell. Yet Emily never said anything of the sort. That was my mistake—thinking she pledged labor or the recuperation of loss or her hand in my hand forever.

What she said was *I love you* and the words sat light as foam on her lip.

When I pull out our pact to point out her breach of contract I'm startled to see my name alone at the bottom of the page. I puzzle over the trick, closing my left eye and then my right.

Her signature is simply not there.

THE AIR IS a haze of pollen and infatuation. Green buds push out from the tips of the Bradford pear tree outside my window. My head is a cracked seed at the edge of explosion. Tight. Wild. Emily and I are six weeks into our affair and for some reason we keep going out with people who cannot be told we're together, even though the secrecy drives me crazy. I keep overestimating my ability to maintain appearances without losing my dignity. I am often plastered and weaving by the end of the night.

Some people turn tables over and break porcelain figures against the walls when they drink. Drinking is a mean streak let loose, an empty vodka bottle, a ready-made excuse. Some people get quiet-drunk and lean into the feeling of falling apart. Swallow pills, let go, stop the heart. Passive-aggressive drinkers move in the opposite direction, letting alcohol firm up their grip. They turn the screw. They twist the knife.

"I think I love you," Emily chants, bobbing up and down next to the stereo. She is singing along with the Partridge Family. The song ends. She plays it again. Something in me tightens. I bore holes in her with my stare. NOTICE ME. I furrow my brow and concentrate, eyes spiraling like augurs through layers of wood and flesh, hesitating just a bit before pushing through the brief bright bone of her skull. I imagine we are Siamese twins separated by surgery at birth. My blood runs in her veins and her blood runs in mine. I touch a hot stove somewhere in another state and her hand burns like she held it in a fire. I wake from a nightmare and her heart races. My tongue is thick with stage fright. Her mouth goes dry. I never even have to say a word. She just knows.

It's not true but I long to be connected like that. I want someone to be able to tell I am out of sorts by the details of my distraction, like leaving the drawers of my dresser cracked open. I want someone to know me as well as Vanessa knows Emily. I am breaking and entering their intimacy. It is the fact of being seen that I want to pocket for my own.

Emily indulges me when it's convenient and ignores me when it's not. She reminds me of a woman who dated my father when I was fifteen. She bought me a padded bra and taught me to drive a stick. She wanted me to like her but I saw her always looking backwards over her shoulder to see if my father had fallen in love yet. I am not her main audience. I do not understand her mixed signals.

Moons rise and set. Climates change. I'm still exactly the same—
Teenager grown woman angry child protest cry.

Emily holds me by the wrists and claps my hands. I don't know how to say it *hurts* or *I want you to stop.*

A woman in pale blue cowboy boots made doe eyes at my father fifteen years ago. She swiveled the ash from her Virginia Slims into the shape of a sharp pencil with its tip on fire. He wasn't in love with her. He was rebuilding something my mother tore down. He wanted to be wanted. I wanted him to be happy again and make jokes in the car instead of listening to jazz trumpets groan and warble while his jaw clenched and unclenched. I wanted to see him happy and silly and filled up and this cowgirl made him smile again so I listened politely and never so much as twitched my lip at the twang of her oval-shaped vowels.

I was fifteen and could not name my emotions if I tried. My poems came out sticky and dark and bizarre—more breakfast club than bell jar—and they all said the same thing.

No one at the table sees me.

> If you are in a relationship where you feel
> great swings in feelings from love to hatred
> and anger, you can be sure that you are trying to
> maintain a relationship without having accepted
> the other person's complexity. Probably you are
> hoping to change the other person, which may be,
> at root, a way of pursuing an old task of trying
> to turn your unsatisfying parents into
> gratifying ones. The intensity of this task and
> the rage that accompanies it can be just as much
> a part of the addictive tie as the loving feelings.
> —Howard Halpern, *How to Break Your Addiction to a Person*

I sit across the room from Emily in a house where no one knows we're together and I am erased by her secrecy. I need her to see me because I am still fifteen / still eleven / still three / a cracked seed.

I WANT TO SHAKE EMILY. I want to leave bruises shaped like question marks on her neck. I want to ask rude questions like *Why are you like this?* I want her to ache with longing for me in the joints of her fingers and the small of her back. I want her to be a million-dollar mansion blazing out of control when the fire could not be contained to the bathtub. I reach into my pocket for a book of matches. I love her with a pyromaniac's passion. I want Emily to burn for me. I want to be a mistake she can never take back.

I distract myself from the disorientation of being Emily's secret by pretending to greet the present moment as if I invited it. Emily steals kisses with me in the stairwell like the party is a Victorian poem. She whispers sweet nothings to me by the kitchen sink and pops an olive in my mouth as she asks me to sleep over. She wants to play a game where we are sisters and one of us is dying and the other one has to kiss her back to life. We draw secrets and promises like fruit-flavored candies from the recesses of our open mouths.

I taste the bitterness of rare pears on my lips.
I should decline her invitation but I don't.

The evening wears on and on. I wait to be claimed and each hour weighs heavier than the last. I want to tell Emily I am dying for real and she must step in immediately to save me. I send this message to her with my powers of mental telepathy but she averts her eyes.

Oh! I say to myself. *I get it.*

The wine turns sour in my mouth so I fill a fresh glass with straight bourbon.

I'm NOT GOOD ENOUGH to be her real romantic partner. I'm NOT GOOD ENOUGH to introduce as her girlfriend. I'm just the second best girl you pull into the corner when no one is looking.

I hate her for a minute.

———————

Emily rejects my self-loathing with the wave of a hand and a smile as fast as a fox, but nothing she says can stop me from using the NOT GOOD ENOUGH story to confirm every negative thing I ever thought about myself.

TOXIC. UNWANTED.

He's not even your real father.

When the party ends I point my car towards home and drive too fast towards the beach, flushed with wine and shame and secrecy and sudden clarity. *I have to get away from her. I have to get out of here.*

Picture me standing on a beach with Emily and drawing a line in the sand with the sharp edge of a broken shell.

Picture me writing UNACCEPTABLE on Emily's side of the line.

That's what driving home felt like. Something broken and hollow in my hand. A deep groove in the sand. Leaving is my most practiced psychological defense—sudden, manic, and laced with persecutory anxiety—the disappearing act.

The one where I am suddenly gone.

Out the door like Johnny Paycheck.

I mobilize my inner resources to stand up for better emotional labor conditions. I am the protestor, the protested, and the sign of protest itself.

> Take this job and shove it.
>
> I ain't working here no more.

By tomorrow I will become the scab. *I'm just glad for a paycheck in the right-to-work state of this relationship,* I will say. *Times are hard all around,* I'll say, but even I won't believe my rationalizations. I'll sling my arms out at my sides like I mean this whole upset apple cart world—from South Carolina to the flaming tip of Tierra del Fuego— like we are all in a land of fire and everyone on this planet is ready to STOP, DROP, AND ROLL just like me. *This is about survival.* I will already be walking away from the camera when I yell my last words in the direction of my imaginary interviewer.

> *People do what they have to do.*

When I get home, I call Emily.

> The neurotic expects to rid herself of
> the consequences of her unresolved conflicts
> without changing anything inside her at all.

I can't end the affair but I won't swallow the humiliation that comes with it.

I live inside this contradiction like city dwellers live in small towns.

I manage. I make do. I sort through a shelf of brown lettuce in Bi-Lo muttering *I hate this place* under my breath.

> As a rule, the relationship from which she expects
> heaven on earth only plunges her into deeper misery.
> She is all too likely to carry her conflicts into the
> relationship and thereby destroy it. Even the most
> favorable possibility can relieve only the actual
> distress; unless her conflicts are resolved her
> development will still be blocked.

We spend most of the night on the phone—lying in the separate bedrooms of the separate houses of our separate lives—both of us staring into space in silence.

I HOLD MY BREATH in the morning shower while warm water streams on to my face. I rub my eyes and wet my hair, scratch shampoo into my scalp, then scrub the skin on my arms and legs with a rough ocean sponge to urge opiates from my nervous system. I want endorphins and enkephalins with my coffee to take the sting of self-deprivation from my eyes.

It's time to give my weekly lecture in a survey class on American literature. I suit up for my off-off-broadway performance of a woman supposed by other people to know something about something. I wear my merino wool blazer like a breastplate. I need to feel safe. ARMORED.

I walk into the room already lecturing.

I reach the front of the room and turn to face a long wall of white boards where I map out the meaning of a famous short story by Herman Melville in purple marker ink. The story is a study in dissatisfaction published in 1853 called *Bartleby, the Scrivener,* about a man who takes a boring and mindless job copying legal briefs in a lawyer's office. The other staff members—an alcoholic and a neurotic—are obnoxious and the lawyer leads with a weak hand.

The line everyone remembers from this story belongs to Bartleby. "I would prefer not to," he says in response to every request. He bobs up and down and pushes repeat. Like a girl with an eating disorder, all his power lies in saying no. He makes an art of disguised refusal. His NO wears the wig and dark sunglasses of preference. He hides his NO underneath the knife, gun, pepper spray, garbage bags, and rubber tubing in the trunk. His life is a love poem to a man who doesn't want him anymore.

The poem consists of one word. NO.

The lawyer has no idea how to respond to Bartleby's refusal to play his assigned social role. He is weak and confused, and students despise him. I think the lawyer and I are kindred spirits. He ignores and cajoles. He pleads. *He yells.* HE STEPS BACK. Like a lesbian one-night-stand, he invites Bartleby to move in with him. Bartleby prefers not to. The lawyer asks Bartleby to be a little reasonable but Bartleby prefers not be reasonable. Scholars of literature have diagnosed Bartleby as depressed and possibly autistic. No one has yet pointed out the PATHOGENIC ENVIRONMENT that draws out Bartleby's crazy side. For one thing the lawyer is a drama queen. He calls the police, who then cart Bartleby to jail, where he prefers not to eat. Bartleby grows thin and then thinner. Eventually his lungs prefer not to breathe.

Most people don't see Bartleby as a teenage girl like I do.

Most people don't see NO as the answer to the meaning of life.

The story is usually taught as a comment on the demoralizing rise of industrial capitalism—the long hours, repetitive stress injuries, tight quarters and unforgiving chairs, the mindless work, the interchangeable workers, the alienation of human labor—and I dutifully chart the readings of Bartleby as Melville's interruption of capitalism's dehumanizing instrumentalist values. YOU ARE WHAT YOU DO. A GOOD MAN IS A GOOD WORKER. He saves money and complaints for his family. Or he saves them for the weekend and spends them on whiskey and whores.

My students are fervent instrumentalists who take Bartleby preferring not to as a pansy-assed abdication of responsibility. They want a world that makes easy sense. They want a good grade in this class and a college degree for a job and an income and a retirement account. They are not here for the subtle highs of ambiguity like Demerol taking top off the top of my head.

I crave questions without answers and stories that are not what they seem on the surface. *I don't know what good is,* I imagine myself saying, *and neither do you.* I want to say *Most of us know good like newborns know words. Blurred tones. Air, lips, saliva. Frustration.* I want to scream, *I am being consumed by a romance with a woman who will not claim me as her lover in front of other people. I am sleeping with her even though she belongs to someone else.*

I want to tell them this is what Bartleby and all great literature is about.

THE FACT THAT I'M NOT A GOOD PERSON.

I want to tell them I carve scarlet letters in my skin like hate mail in the dead letter office of my body. *They pile up over time,* the lawyer says of the dead letters at the post office where Bartleby once worked, *and are burned by the cartload. When I think of this loss I can hardly express the emotions that seize me.* I share his distress over the idea of misdirected messages—MISSIVES PARDONING THOSE WHO DIED DESPAIRING, ENVELOPES BEARING RINGS FOR FINGERS MOLDING IN THE GRAVE, WORDS OF RELIEF FOR THOSE WHO DIED STIFLED BY UNRELIEVED CALAMITIES—and I too want to return to the errands of life and stop calling things by the wrong name.

I want to say my apartment is no paradise for bachelorettes and would be more accurately described by terms like PAIN CLINIC,

WOUND-CARE CENTER, or HALFWAY HOUSE for the chronically triggered, the emotionally dysregulated, the bright but broken-hearted,
and a few repeat offenders of adulterous behavior. This space is no
disco. The décor is sparse, its blank white walls punctuated with
phrases like CUNNING, BAFFLING, AND POWERFUL, cross-stitched and
framed for the residents.

I want to say her words are wrong.

I turn my back to my students and recite the unspoken words of
the lawyer as he tries to read Bartleby and fails.

"He calls Bartleby an inscrutable text," I say. I write INSCRUTABLE
in tall aubergine letters on the board. I stare at the term in awe. "This
is not a story about preferences," I say. I face the class, close the book,
and ground my point in the audacity of softened speech. "This is a story
about not knowing the right thing to do." I search the blurred frustrated
faces in front of me. "This is a story," I say, watching for signs of epiph-
any or protest in their expressions, "about not being able to understand
someone." Some students listen closely and nod with encouragement.
Others perch with packed book-bags, one foot pointing towards the
door. They already know more than I know.

Bartleby and the lawyer deserve each other.
If either of them really wanted happiness he would grow a spine
and stop wasting time talking to someone who will never understand him.

When Emily calls me in the car on my way home from campus I shriek with delight into the phone. "You called!" I emote. "I didn't think you would call!"

"I miss you," she says in a soft narcotic voice. "I can think of nothing but you."

"My darling!" I say.

At home I peel wool from my body, wash sweat from my face, and wipe traces of red lipstick from the corners of my mouth. I wear pink slippers and drink red wine and fall into a deep blue sea of dreamless sleep.

SPRING ENDS and has neither killed me nor made me stronger.

The month of May is my break from the classroom. I relish the freedom to read whatever I want. What I want to read are AIDS memoirs. I am comforted by their treatments of grief. I am on a vision quest. I am on a long train of thought.

I sit still in the lizard cold of the air conditioning. I fall into a physical torpor. The scoliosis twist and rotation soon radiate pain through my legs and hips and back. I am lurching towards the bathroom like an old lady when my muscles make a violent revolt. Seized by panic and spasm and collapse. I crawl to the phone and wait for the permission of first light and pink dawn sky.

I call Emily and tell her I can't stand on my feet.

She becomes my EMERGENCY CONTACT.

EMILY comes over the next night and cooks me dinner but I can't eat. The hot prickling inflammation of my sacroiliac joints feels like a form of need. I need her. The need tastes like metal.

"I'm going to lose you," I say. "Everything's going to change." I am not asking for reassurance. I want to make her tell me the terrible truth. I want to make her admit it will hurt.

"I will still love you," she murmurs in my ear. "That won't change." She stands beside my chair and wraps me in her arms.

"I don't know what that means," I say.

The top of my head aches from the pressure of her chin. I close my eyes and do not ask her to move.

EMILY sends a bouquet of hot pink rosebuds the next day and I skip past I LOVE YOU to the blank space where her name should be. I squint at the small white rectangle marked with her message—XOXO— and I sound out its curves and slashes in the slow vowels of speech after a stroke.

"ZOH . . . ZOH . . ."

I want it to be Sanskrit for You possess me. Or some ancient symbol used by women in love with each other as a vow of loyalty that loosely translates as *I will call your name in public for all the world to hear and they will know I love you and you will know it and all manner of things will be well.* I picture it tattooed in a trail down my spine. I need the message to mean something. I need it to be real.

But the word that is not a word slips stupidly from my mouth.

Even the oily stain it leaves on the floor is something I imagine.

THE GIFT OF SELF-DESTRUCTION

THE COMPLEX OF MELANCHOLIA BEHAVES LIKE
AN OPEN WOUND, DRAWING TO ITSELF CATHECTIC
ENERGY FROM ALL SIDES AND DRAINING THE
EGO UNTIL IT IS UTTERLY DEPLETED.
—SIGMUND FREUD, "Mourning and Melancholia"

I TELL EMILY WE'RE OVER THE DAY BEFORE VANESSA MOVES BACK IN.

I cry into the carpet until it leaves burn marks on my forehead. I hold on to the floor like it's moving, like I might fall through it. A load-bearing structure in my psyche has collapsed and I have no idea why. I feel desperate. Something has come unhinged inside me. I walk gingerly in the grocery store, leaning on the cart for support. I drive myself to the chiropractor's office, to the gym, to the bar. I push thumbtacks through a note in the center of my bulletin board where I have carefully printed my new emotional policy.

NO WISTFULNESS. But I am wistful.

WISTFULNESS sounds like a wilted emotion, a bit of lavender pressed between the pages of a well-tempered personality. At worst the SHRINK-ING VIOLET makes a wet spot where words bleed through. But wistfulness is no wallflower. She is the quiet psychosis of still waters. She twists raw fingers in her hair. She leaps high in the air with harm in one hand and reward in the other and no grip left for nightmares.

She is a BAD SEED. She sleeps naked. She rides bareback.

Neuropsychiatry calls this recklessness a fatal flaw.
GO FASTER. SCARE ME.

Ann Marlowe was a high-functioning heroin addict. In her memoir of addiction she describes the drug as a way to stop time. She calls the high "a stand-in, a stop-gap, a mask, for what we believe is missing." Addiction is the kissing cousin of nostalgia. They pass for sisters in a certain light. Each time the addict uses, she gestures backwards to the perfect unrecoverable past, reaching for something she can never have again. "The chemistry of the drug is ruthless: it is designed to disappoint you," Marlowe says. Likewise, cultural anthropologists say the biochemistry of love is addictive. When a person becomes infatuated, her body floods with chemicals that stimulate the brain with a natural form of speed. The user always wants more. "[T]he romance junkie swings from feeling brokenhearted and desperately depressed," says Helen Fisher, "to feeling elated over each inappropriate, ill-fated romantic fling."

"Barriers also seem to provoke this madness," she writes. "THE CHASE." Affairs with unavailable people are a heroin high before nausea hits. Like smack they are destined to disappoint.

They begin with magic. *Then the chasing after magic.*

And finally the MOURNING FOR MAGIC.

I MAKE A BEELINE for the west coast. I think about Emily and Vanessa locked in a glowing embrace and I want to be very far away. I visit my friend Lila in Los Angeles. We go on adventures. We find treasures. I tell Lila I want a girlfriend like her with a clavicle you could drown in. I put my arm around her as we look out at the ocean. I look at the endless green sea and choose grief over dread. I kiss Lila on the lips. We bar hop a bit, then stop the car somewhere in West Hollywood and have sex in the front seat. As she puts her tiny car in drive again and pulls away from the curb, I watch the traffic lights blink yellow through Lila's toe prints like daisy petals on the windshield.

I want to forget Emily. I want to be over her.

My life has been reduced to a frantic effort to hold Emily
HOSTAGE-CLOSE.

I have thought of ending the affair only in terms of loss. The embarrassment of a ribbon printed in gold with the title RUNNER-UP. I am haunted by the idea that QUITTERS NEVER WIN and WINNERS NEVER QUIT. I consider the maniac pace of emailing and texting and calling, the unrelenting focus of seduction and rivalry. And for an instant, I glimpse it—not what stopping takes away but what stopping could provide—the deep pool calm of a quiet mind. I miss the stillness of long unworried reflection.

I want it back almost as much as I want Emily.

"I knew you'd sleep with her," Emily says when she picks me up at the airport. She would never charge me with betrayal. She knows she has no right. Still I am anxious in the light of her disapproval. Whether it's fair or not. Whether it's there or not. I am on the hot seat and the truth is I'm glad for the heat.

She cares. This still matters to me.

Why does obsession open like a blister on my face?

What makes the difference between THRIVING and FAILING TO THRIVE?

One girl scars from cigarette burns on her back, her arm broken in the shape of her mother's ruthless grip. Her face is a calm ocean and she never even looks at the faded pink moons of tissue along her scapula. Another girl is cut in half by a sharp look. When she loses her head she points fingers instead of picking it up. One person places love like a stone at each corner of her lover's body. Another trails it in the wisp and blur of white lies. It dribbles from her lips and fingertips. It garbles her words.

Why do I want her?

The genes of two alcoholic grandfathers and two addict parents flooded the sac of amniotic fluid that held me nine months inside my mother's body. The acid of self-sabotage braised my fetus limbs. I fermented. I squirmed from my mother's birth canal already high and screaming for comfort. My attachment bonds fit in the hand like a small glass pipe—hot to the lips and easy to hide—a hand-blown one-hitter with scarlet ribbons wriggling down the center. *If I get stoned and sing all night long,* well, no one could say they didn't see it coming.

I spent my early childhood in a state of chronic anxiety. I wrote love notes to each parent and from the time I could put words to paper I packaged my affection with uncertainty.

> I love you Linda. I like you. Do you love me Do you like me Linda Yes I no you do Linda. I love you Linda and Marty I Like You Do you love me Do you like me Yes I no you do Linda and Marty. Happy Mother's Day I love you mom [and do you love me]

Questions itched in hard to reach places.

Children with insecure attachment styles are bad to chase the dragon. We become addicted to our own adrenaline and we always go back for more—no matter how dangerous the dose or how blue the comedown. The memory of intense psychological arousal *I love you do you love me* leaves us with a craving for powerful jolts.

> I HOLD *LOVE* ON THE BACK OF MY TONGUE, BITTER PILL OF A WORD, BITTER AS POISON, DETERMINED TO DIE RATHER THAN SPIT IT OUT. THAT'S JUST HOW CRAZY I AM.
> —NANCY MAIRS,
> *Remembering the Bone House:*
> *An Erotics of Place and Space*

A new crush texts. A co-worker loops a pinky finger over yours.
The perfect fit as opiate and tourniquet.

A GAL COULD GET HOOKED ON THIS FEELING.

IN THE STEAMING HEAT of June we are fast storms and loud
thunderclaps. We cannot give each other more than a day or two of
peace at a time. We call and say mean things *I thought you loved me! You
don't even know what the word means!* and hang up on each other like
thirteen-year-olds.

I want Emily to acknowledge the choice she has made. She says
I am the one making the choice by insisting we are ALL or NOTHING.
I wedge words like SIGNIFICANT OTHER and PRIMARY PARTNER between
her lips but she spits them out unformed in my face. We are hot and
cold. We cross paths on purpose. We generate reasons to test the water
but we are looking for different things. She checks the gauge for FRIENDS
or LOVERS. I read the meter for LOVERS or ENEMIES.

Vanessa leaves town again for six weeks midsummer.
Emily finds a house for me to buy in her neighborhood. I move in.

For six weeks we suspend all rules of morality and let ourselves revel in wanton behaviors. We take hot showers together and drink bourbon together and lie in the wet grass kissing each other while spiders bite our thighs and backs. Her teenage daughter peers into the dark yard and dials her other mother's number to tell her it's still going on.

We give in to whatever this is. We want more. We are speed freaks who want to keep going. *It doesn't even feel good.* The dope used to be the means to a euphoric end. Now the point of the dope is the dope.

> Addictive relationships are marked by their endurance.
> We are prepared to lie, cheat, and steal from other people.
> We begin to lie, cheat, and steal from each other. In the
> face of decreasing pleasure and even intense painfulness.
> —Stanton Peele, "Fools for Love: The Romantic Ideal,
> Psychological Theory and Addictive Love"

Emily halfway agrees to rid herself of Vanessa to make room for our growing addiction. I halfway pretend to believe her.

The lie we collude in is not yet.

We will be together but not yet.

We will be together but first this.

The relationship with Vanessa must be brought gradually to an end. Emily needs time for a graceful goodbye. I look at the academic calendar and count nine months between this NOT YET and the supposed eventual YES.

I USED TO BELIEVE people who ran out of rooms before bursting into tears were being intentionally melodramatic. Now I become one of those people. I am so brittle I feel like I might break into pieces if someone looks too hard in my direction. I am holding on to sanity like a window ledge I fell out of. I become obsessed with Emily's sleeping arrangements. I ask questions, wanting clarity about something. The questions pry my fingers one by one from the ledge.

"Do you still sleep in the same bed?"

"Do you spoon with her?"

"Do you ever, in a dreamy lazy early morning sleep,
sling your leg over her body? Or let her sling a leg over yours?"

Psychologists call it PERSEVERATION.

I call it EMOTIONAL SELF-CUTTING.

Searching out a painful image, going over it and over it in my mind, raking its sharp edges over my open psychological sores. My mind generates the million and one questions I ask in order to avoid asking the only one that matters. *Can you save me?*

At the time I believe my thoughts are real.

I believe I'm solving something.

> ONE RESPONSE TO FEELING ABANDONED
> IS TO ABANDON YOURSELF.
> —THEODORE MILLON, *Personality Disorders in Modern Life*

I stop eating.

I am experimenting with deprivation as a way of protesting Emily's intermittent availability. I think of it at the time as an act of sadness but I will later realize the truth about eating disorders and cutting and alcoholism and the logic that structures every form of self-injury. Living in a house without heat is a sustained act of hostility. Not eating is a test of endurance. I can go without so many things. This wilderness skill keeps me safe. I short-circuit my needs and defuse other people's power over me.

I want to defy trauma.

I picture myself monstrous and strange, like the day I climbed from the broken window of a wrecked car in shock, bleeding from my torn cheek and coughing up glass on the sparkling asphalt.

When I feel hunger signs again—a headache, nausea—I let anxiety push it away.

I open the refrigerator, then close it. Late evening I give in, pour a bowl of cereal or steam a serving of broccoli. I don't want flavor or a full stomach. I want someone to take care of me. Someone should be paying closer attention.

I'm not okay.

The goal of maintaining mental wellness really can be measured in units of OKAYNESS. When I'M OKAY and YOU'RE OKAY, everyone is in her right mind and life can be met as a manageable challenge. Two adults communicate clearly with each other and observe appropriate roles and boundaries. These are complementary transactions.

Problems crop up when the wires get crossed. Two adults speak to each other but one adopts the prescriptive voice of a parent rather than a peer. If the other one follows suit and responds in the helpless voice of a child, the OKAYNESS of the room loses balance. Crossed transactions hook the ego state of the child buried inside the adult. Next thing you know, the adultchild sits in a cold room dripping tears on an empty table.

> THE PERSON WHOSE NOT OK CHILD IS
> ALWAYS ACTIVATED CANNOT GET ON
> WITH TRANSACTIONS WHICH WILL ADVANCE
> HIS DEALING WITH REALITY BECAUSE
> HE IS CONTINUALLY CONCERNED WITH UNFINISHED
> BUSINESS HAVING TO DO WITH A PAST REALITY.
> —THOMAS HARRIS, *I'm Okay, You're Okay*

Emily drops by one evening and finds me crying in the kitchen.

"It's cold in here."

I am wearing a long sleeved T-shirt, a thin silk cardigan, a wool cardigan, and a fleece jacket zipped up beneath my chin.

"I know," I say.

She tells me to get in the car. She has something to show me. She rides me around a nearby neighborhood, takes me on a tour of the Christmas lights, shows me yards in the lower middle class area a few blocks from my house filled with enormous sleighs, reindeer, and snowmen, all lit up, with moving parts and sound effects. Santa waves, lithium lidded, as we pass by. I look out the window of the car and cry harder. The blue and green and red and white blur and grow faint as we turn the corner back on to the highway. I hate this scene of manufactured sentimentality. I want her to stop handing me postcards and platitudes.

In my kitchen again, Emily says, "What can I do? Why aren't you happy? You should be enjoying your wonderful house, your solitude. What I would give for your solitude. I wish I lived here." I look at Emily, my chest tight with resentment towards families and holiday lights and joy. I am outside the magic circle.

"So do I."
I'm not sure if I mean I wish she lived here or I wished I lived here.

"Seriously, what's wrong?"

"I'm lonely."
I am regressing. Refusing to do for myself.

That night Emily turns the heat on and leaves a box of Italian chocolates at my house. I unwrap one after she goes home, breaking my hunger strike with one decadent bite, and as I savor the rich dark flavor I read the quotation on the wax paper inside. It is from the eighteenth century French philosopher Denis Diderot.

There is only one passion, the passion for happiness.

Emily brings food over in plastic containers the next day. I scoop warm couscous into my mouth after she leaves. I want food only if it comes from her hand. I want warmth only if she sets the thermostat herself. I have chosen to respond as the child and my playful reenactment quickly hardens into habit. I forget how to respond adult-to-adult.

My NOT-OKAY child is a beanstalk. She grows like corn in the night. She pokes her pink sausage wonderland arms out the windows of my little house.

ONE NIGHT I WAKE from a bad dream and call Emily moaning *I need you* into the phone like an accusation. I want her to make an honest woman of me. She says she doesn't know what I mean.

"I love you—can't you see that?" and her meaningless words tap inarticulate as rain on tin. I stop speaking and make the low mournful noises of a dog left outside in a thunderstorm.

"There's nothing anyone can do," I say. I press the edges of my teeth into the bony curve of my kneecap. Emily drives to my house and crawls into bed to lick my wounds. I rock and pant and spit glass at her feet.

Thin wet dogs come to me in my dreams.

I don't know how to help them.

"You are driving me crazy," I wail. *"Why don't you care?"* The last word—C A R E—loses elasticity and flattens into another long wail. I am knees on the floor, shoulders on the floor, forehead on the floor. It is the fetal position. I get caught in a loop of feelings. I get louder and louder. I am groping about for the concept of NEGLECT. She is neglecting me. But I can't find the words. I can't catch my breath.

"I DON'T KNOW WHAT TO DO," she says.

This time she does not come to me so I break up with Emily (again). This time when she tells me it's killing her I don't respond in my usual way. I tell her I can't help her. I tell her to try therapy.

I need therapy too.

Other people would confidently end such a relationship based on the obvious logic of infidelity—if she cannot be TRUE BLUE to her partner, she will not be TRUE BLUE to you—but I resist this logic. I moon and sob and swear to god Emily's simply amazing. I sulk and whine.

I want THE AMAZING EMILY for my own.

"THIS PART SHOULD be over by now," Paula says, "but you are frozen in the infatuation stage because you cannot move forward in the normal way in this relationship." She watches my face for cracks but I'm sealed tight. "You should be having the power struggle by now. You should be seeing each other as real people by now. But you're not. No wonder you're confused and exhausted. She remains the sought-after illusion for you. None of this is real."

I won't concede the point. I insist it's real. I think Paula can't help me because Paula doesn't get our passion. I don't even really want her to. I just want her to supervise my withdrawal from the drug.

"I'm not going to tell you not to see her," Paula said. "That's not my job. That's not what I'm here for." I walk across the hot asphalt to my car, slam the door, and turn the music up too loud. Soon I am running my hands over Emily's body in remote corners of empty parking lots.

I'M A BEAST . . .

I GO MAD . . .

All I want from therapy is a boost out of my enmeshed state. Not big picture therapeutic work. A BAND-AID, a BLOW-POP, and an UPBEAT PROGNOSIS. When I don't get a quick fix I drop out.

> The Child wants immediate results:
>
> Instant coffee.
>
> Thirty-second waffles.
>
> Immediate relief.

Emily and I are stuck in this ambivalent embrace. We don't want to go forward or backward. We just want to stay here like this. We want to die like this. Sometimes I turn on her with vicious accusations. You come to my house and fill your mouth with figs. *You use me to satisfy your pleasures, then send me to bed without supper.* Sometimes I offer her everything I have. Time. Money. My kidney. I tell her I want to live together and parent her child like a real couple.

Somehow she knows none of this is true. I don't.

I believe whatever I say, whatever I decide, can be true if I try hard enough.

And I vow to make it all true.

THE ADDICT, OF COURSE, CANNOT BE TRUSTED.

I WILL SAY ANYTHING TO GET WHAT I WANT.

YOU WOULD BE WELL ADVISED NOT TO BELIEVE HIM IF HE SAYS HE WILL LEAVE HIS MARRIAGE AND WILL BE WITH YOU IF HE HAS MADE NO MOVES TO CHANGE HIS STATUS, NO MATTER HOW LOVING HE IS. IF YOU ARE CAUGHT IN A BIND LIKE THIS, IT IS IMPORTANT THAT YOU RECOGNIZE THE HARD TRUTH THAT HE HAS ATTACHMENT HUNGER NEEDS SO GREAT THAT HE IS TRYING TO HOLD ONTO BOTH HIS SPOUSE AND YOU. IF HE DOES NOT WANT TO END HIS MARRIAGE, THE MOST MATURELY LOVING THING HE COULD DO FOR YOU WOULD BE TO COMPLETELY, UNCONDITIONALLY, AND IRREVOCABLY GET OUT OF YOUR LIFE. IT IS NOT LOVE BUT SELF-INDULGENCE THAT LEADS HIM TO HANG IN THERE, FEEDING YOU THE POISONED SWEETS OF FALSE HOPE.

—HOWARD HALPERN,

How to Break Your Addiction to a Person

I join a long history of lady-loving-ladies feasting on rare pears of fantasy. We reenact *The Well of Loneliness* as if torture came like a toaster with our jacket for members only. We are lesbians who languish. Emily plays Angela. I play Stephen.

> *Stephen was blinded by stardust and love stories.*
> *Stephen saw perfection where none existed.*
> *Stephen saw patience that was purely fictitious.*
> *Stephen conceived of a loyalty far beyond*
> *the limits of Angela's nature.*

I think she would be with me if she could. I think she's stuck.

I yell down into the tight space where she's wedged, *Hold on, I'm coming!* I lie down by the edge of the well and talk gently in the voice of a dreamer.

I try to put her in a trance.

> *Because we love each other so deeply. Because we're*
> *perfect, a perfect thing, you and I. Because we're not two*
> *separate people but one. Because our love has lit a great*
> *comforting beacon, so that we need never be afraid of the*
> *dark anymore. We can warm ourselves at our love.*

My face is hot. I am sitting in front of a fire.

All Emily gave seemed the gift of love and all Emily withheld seemed withheld out of honor. *If only I were free,* she was always saying. *But I can't just leave Vanessa.* Then I would feel ashamed of my inner Stephen and humble myself to the very dust.

The heroine hates you, I want to shout at that former affair-bound self. *The drug is destined to disappoint!*

Stephen went and knelt beside her. She cried like a child. Angela was stirred to something like love. Don't cry honey, we're together, she says. Nothing else really matters. And so it began all over again.

ONE AFTERNOON Emily and I see a movie about two men who love each other but will not claim this love in public. After the credits roll, we walk into the afternoon light with our hands over our eyes. We drive back to my house and talk about the film—the blood-spattered murder scene, the brutal tenderness of Heath Ledger's shoulders and eyes, the stupid brouhaha over gay cowboy sex—all nervous chatter to avoid talking about our own brokenness.

I extend my hand and draw Emily to the floor between our chairs.

We press against each other, pull at each other's clothing, breathe into each other's hair. Rubbing against her body is like breaking open the leaves of a poisonous plant. Welts rise up in red blotches on the surface of my psyche. My eyes swell shut.

This is the last time, I think to myself.

I think about something Emily told me after Valentine's Day. She had given her teenage daughter a one-pound bag of candy and Jade ate the whole bag in one night. I feel angry with Emily for giving her daughter the whole bag of candy and expecting her to not to eat it. Now I am the teenaged daughter and Emily has handed me the whole bag of candy. I have gorged myself on her and I feel sluggish and ill.

Why does she keep letting me make myself sick on her? Underneath this thought, I know what is really true. I am not a teenager. I am not her daughter. It is up to me to say no. To say I've had enough.

I tell her I'm getting sicker and sicker. I tell her it has to stop. My voice is thin and broken. I can barely make myself say the words.

"I'm not eating. I have a headache all the time. I can't think about anything but you. I can barely prepare to teach my classes. I'm at the end of my rope, and I have to stop." I say this in a pleading voice, wanting her to understand.

"This is not what I want, but if it's what you need, I will do it." She doesn't want me to think it is easy for her or that she doesn't care. But we are both tired.

I give us both another lie for consolation:

This is not the end. This is not forever.

We agree (again) to stop seeing each other until she finalizes her separation from Vanessa. My feelings for her are slowly changing from the long wait. Instead of admiration and euphoria, I am weighed down with anger and insecurity. I resent Emily for enjoying the benefits of attachment while refusing the obligations of relationship. I resent myself for going along with this bad bargain. Even though I strained and choked on my request for a cleaner break, I am light with relief when I leave her office. The movements of my limbs are more coordinated, relieved from the tension of watching for texts proclaiming her abiding love or announcing she will swing by for a brandy.

I'd rather cut contact than keep waiting and wondering.

I once read a story about a Puritan woman in Colonial America who became so crazed by waiting to find out if she was among the elect—the ones who go to heaven in the afterlife—she threw her infant daughter into a well to die.

Just so she could stop wondering where she will end up.

Hell it is, she decided for herself.

Here is what is hardest to explain.

I CHOOSE HELL AGAIN AND AGAIN.

I break up with Emily more times than I remember—my reconstructed timeline is a tedious report of the days and reasons for each decision to split—but we never follow through with the plan to stop seeing each other. We never run out of excuses or holidays or alibis or lies. We never pull back long enough to detox. Just long enough for the most acute symptoms of addiction to subside. I am thoroughly engaged by this game of EAT YOUR HEART OUT. I can't stop throwing my organs like playing cards on the table and yelling at Emily when she tries to pick them up. She is my attachment fetish figure and I want to bind us together at the wrists and ankles. If I can make her love me, a door will fly open and I will enter a world where I am always safe and warm and full. She is KEY and DOOR and WORLD and MEAL after savory meal. She is RESCUE and EMERGENCY and PYRO and SIREN. She is MOON and LADDER and ENDLESS SKY OF WANTING.

I write her into every possible role in my fantasies of belonging and escape. I love her and hate her. I make her up from scratch. We are on again off again like a spinning ball of light. I court her with the inconstant postures of the epileptic.

The question of how to remove the fishhook of obsession from my own open eye will follow me long after I leave Emily for good. A year after leaving Emily, I will lie in bed draining cognac straight from the bottle, and I will stand up to go to the bathroom only to surprise myself by slamming my fist into the full-length mirror on my wall. I will hit it over and over, disconcerted when it doesn't break.

I drunk text her—*It's still you. For me.*—then fall into bed and sleep.

> ALL I KNOW IN LOVE IS HOW TO SHOCK PEOPLE.
> TO BRIEFLY WORSHIP,
> AND THEN TO DESTROY
> AND BE DESTROYED.
> —LISA CARVER,
> *Drugs Are Nice: A Post-Punk Memoir*

EVEN A SINGLE phone call from Emily easily plunges me back into the confused mindset of hope laced with arsenic. I am pulled apart by the vague pressures of free-floating depression. I watch movies all day in the dark. I only leave my bedroom for more tea. I eat three bananas—breakfast, lunch, dinner—piling brown peels on the bedside table.

"What is wrong with me?" I say to my therapist.

"She hooks you." She makes her hand into the shape of a hook.

"She communicates with you on all these different levels, so that on one level what you hear is that you are loved for who you are no matter what, and that it is okay if you are in a bad mood because everyone has bad moods sometimes and it doesn't have to be a big deal. On another level, what you hear is that you are not important enough to hold her attention and you are not special enough for her to want to let other people know you are in her life."

My therapist specializes in the neuropsychology of communication, and she tells me that when a person receives multiple and conflicting messages from an important figure in her environment, the experience is disorienting. She tells me this is why I feel emotionally dysregulated after I talk to Emily, even when the conversation is mostly easy and fun.

"YES!" I sit up straighter in my chair. "I hear all these different messages, and I tune in especially to the implicit messages, but then I contrast them with the nice spoken ones, and I become obsessed with the work of figuring out what is true, and whether the relationship is good for me or not, and whether I should trust my intuition that it is not good for me, or whether I should grow up and get stronger so that I am less vulnerable to these uncomfortable parts of the relationship."

"There may be a middle path," she says. "Maybe you can just give yourself some time. Maybe you can get to a point where you are less vulnerable to this, but also realize you are not there yet, and that that is okay."

I am still thinking about the disorienting effects of hearing conflicting messages, of being loved and treasured and admired and also neglected and abandoned and kept secret.

"And then," I go on, "I act like this complete crazy person! But the situation MAKES me crazy!"

"When you put an emotionally sensitive person in an invalidating environment," my therapist says, "you bring out her old patterns of reaction. INSECURITY. ANGER. IMPULSIVENESS. Think of all the divorced people who suddenly go crazy. Think of the slashed tires. And the person says afterwards, *I don't know what came over me*."

We are smiling and nodding at each other.

Flash forward for a minute and let me tell you something that happens several years later. I am standing at a street festival in Charlotte, North Carolina—my third Gay Pride celebration of the summer—talking with Yvonne and Bree. We have convened for an afternoon of rainbow stickers and cheap beer in the full sun of late summer. We are making the rounds, reading pithy slogans on buttons and T-shirts along an aisle of vendor booths, and Yvonne stops to speak to someone. She pats her congenially on the shoulder, says, "Hey, girl, what's up?" But the woman she speaks to does not speak back, and Yvonne looks like she's been slapped in the face.

We move on and circle our way back around to the beer booth.

"I cannot believe this," Yvonne says, while I gently tuck the dollar in change down the front of the blouse of the beer vendor. I think for a minute she's talking about my tip but before I can explain that everyone else was putting extra dollars in the V of cleavage, Yvonne says, "That was my ex." Pause. "We just broke up a month ago." Her face looks suddenly younger, gone childlike with insecurity. "We just talked on the phone last week. Her grandmother and my great-aunt both died two weeks ago, and we just talked about it last week." She lets their recent intimacy sink in, then says, "We GRIEVED people together *just last week!*"

"Whoa. That is a bad feeling," I tell her. We are squinting at each other in the brightness of the day.

"I'm going to go over there and ask her why she's acting like this."
"Maybe she's with another girl," Bree offers.

"Well then I'm going to go over there and tell her I don't care who she's with, I still love her. As friends! I'll always love her. You don't just stop caring about someone because you stop dating." Yvonne's words are coming out more indignant than loving right now. "I mean we were together for two years. You don't just stop caring all of a sudden."

"I know how you feel," I say, glancing towards the woman who wouldn't speak, who might be with another girl, who grieved with Yvonne last week. "I know how much you want to go over there and fix it, but let me run another way of looking at it by you." Yvonne and

Bree are both waiting. I am trying to think how to say this without telling them my whole life story.

"The most loving thing you can do right now is give her space. She already indicated she didn't want to talk, so cornering her and trying to make her is just going to push her farther away. That's the surest way to never find out why she's not talking to you right now. She'll get defensive. She'll turn away even more. But if you let her be, she might get to a place over the next few weeks where she feels like she can talk to you again, and you need to give her space so she can come around on her own. And if she doesn't come around, that's about her—that's her stuff—that's not about you or about your value or about what you had or didn't have with her."

"That's amazing. That sounds like my astrology report." She pulls out a folded piece of paper with her horoscope for the day, and it really does say something about giving people space. "How did you learn that?"

"Because I am an obsessor. Because I have tried to fix things." I swallow another mouthful of flat beer. "Because it never worked." I picture my phone hitting the wall, my hand on the razor blade, Emily's initials beading up with blood on my ankle.

"Because I never felt better after acting on my obsessive impulse," I say. "I only ever felt worse. And I wanted to stop feeling worse."

I want to whisper a line of poetry from Rumi in Yvonne's ear. *I have lived on the lip of insanity, wanting to know reasons, knocking on a door.* I remember my body strung tight in the posture of waiting. I remember the metallic taste of separation anxiety filling my mouth with dread.

There is a difference between love and human sacrifice, I imagine saying, but I hold the difference on my tongue and refrain from forcing it into words. My impulse to explain tells me I'm still chasing something, a rush of understanding that continues to elude me. I want to be different but I'm not different yet.

I am using the story of Yvonne to distract you from the snakes in my head—VICIOUS INTROJECTS who drive me crazy with the call to come back for more, to die trying. True as it may be that FANTASIES CAN BE EXAMINED TO DETERMINE WHO IS APPEASED BY INJURY TO THE SELF, and that "THE LINK BETWEEN PRESENT AND PAST CAN BE WEAKENED WITH PENETRATING QUESTIONS LIKE 'DO YOU LOVE THIS PERSON ENOUGH TO GIVE HIM OR HER YOUR SELF-DESTRUCTION?'" the unfortunate fact is this. My answer *(yes, still!)* is so often yes.

Let my mistress call. In the snap of her fingers I become the governor of South Carolina throwing caution to the rip-roaring wind. I slip away from my bodyguards and tell them I'm on a long trail edged with mountain laurel. I tell them I need space. The black suits sulk like a circle of widows. They mourn for me. I am arrow light and crow's flight to my elsewhere in Argentina.

I am another person. I am in another place.

Sometimes you don't choose things. They just happen.

That's what the South American girlfriend said. "I can't redirect my feelings," she said. I want to tell her this is nothing to brag about. I want to tell her you can get help for that. She speaks four languages. She parents two boys. She translates things. Mark Sanford wanted something from her. He made clumsy hearts with threadbare words. *You have grace and calm and curves,* said the smitten kitten politician.

When he gets caught he is a ready confession.

He did not go hiking. He turned his phone off. He disappeared. He crossed lines and he knows this. He cried in a woman's arms for nine days. His wife said his whereabouts were none of her concern. People declared his political future over.

"The writing is on the wall," they said. Still he did not step down.

Before my affair with Emily ends I will lose my equilibrium entirely.

I will cry in front of people I work with. I will inscribe hieroglyphs of loss like teardrop tattoos on my arms and legs. I will spoon secrets from the sockets beneath Emily's closed lids. Scoop morsels of bliss like sweetmeats from her open bowels and offer them back to her as gourmet treats.

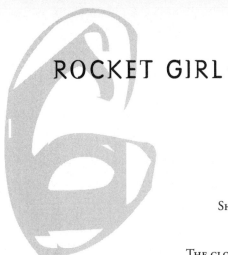

ROCKET GIRL

I think Amelia had it okay
She had a one in a million bad day
With her eyes in the clouds
The clouds in her eyes in a big, wide sky
Expecting to fly
Doesn't sound so bad to me.
—Deb Talan, "Thinking Amelia"

THE NIGHT PRINCESS DIANA died I watched MSNBC straight through to morning. It was August 31, 1997, and I was alone in a small apartment above a house where a family lived. I spent that night on the couch with cool air from the open windows raising goose bumps on my legs. An orange and white cat slept on my chest while I waited for more news and thought about my boyfriend, who moved to Idaho three months ago to begin a very long adventure that would never end with him marrying me.

I watched Diana's face in old footage and she was always Mona Lisa calm. I didn't know her secrets. I didn't know this translucent reed of royalty starved her body and used the serrated edge of a lemon slicer to break the surface of her skin. I didn't know she threw her body into a glass curio cabinet. I had no frame of reference to understand the scene of the car crash that killed her—splintering into glass and metal and bone and blood in a Paris tunnel—as a scene of self-mutilation. Later I will learn about her affairs with the bodyguard and the riding instructor and her demanding ways of romance and friendship. How she begged and pleaded and cried and screamed at people. How she called six times in a row.

Diana tried to help people stop flying apart from stepping on land mines and losing their arms and legs and fingers in Africa and Bosnia. But she also drove people crazy. She was flying apart too. SHE WAS SUR-PRISE BLASTS AND BLOODY STUMPS TOO.

———————

THE DAY AFTER Emily tells me she needs space and I wage war on the doors of my kitchen cabinets until I collapse and cut my ankle, I return to therapy with my tail between my legs. I make my way tentatively into the small room where Paula meets her clients and sit down on the uncomfortable, squishy loveseat. I think a seat with no support is a strange paradox for a therapist's office but I never say anything about it. I just position throw pillows behind me to manage the discomfort in my lower back. I don't event want to look her in the eye. I'm embarrassed to have gone missing since late September. I'm embarrassed to tell her what happened last night.

I quickly explain this isn't me.

I haven't done anything like this since I was a teenager and a boy I liked rejected me at the skating rink. I watched him couple-skating with another girl while I traced the lines on the palm of my hand with a piece of the bathroom mirror another girl shattered with her fist the night before.

I was just thinking about cutting. I hadn't decided to do it yet. I was just thinking it would show him how much it hurt me to be put aside.

Steel guitar thrummed in my chest.

YOU GIVE LOVE A BAD NAME.

The song ended and I looked down at the inside of my hand to find my palm covered in the trickling red lines of back roads on a rural map.

I was fourteen. It was an accident.

And then I couldn't stop.

I tell Paula about the phone and the wall and Emily's initials in my flesh. I show Paula my ankle.

The first day I met Paula she said she thought she knew what was up with me. I wanted her to tell me right that minute. If there was a word for my problem of falling into a black hole when I break up with someone and feeling like I might never find my way back to gravity and ground beneath my feet, I wanted to know that word. She steered me away from words and asked me to look inside instead. All I could see when I looked inside was obsession like a mass in my chest. Nothing else mattered. Then it dawns on me.

She thinks I'm CODEPENDENT.

Big deal. I've known this since AlaTeen.

Daughter of an addict, history of having trouble ending bad relationships—blah blah blah—so let's get started. I'LL BE CODEPENDENT NO MORE. I announce my insight at the next session, but Paula says, "Aren't all women codependent to some degree or another?"

I want her to spill the beans but she won't.

I want her to play obsession police but she won't.

When my divorce twelve years earlier left me depressed and dysregulated—when I couldn't read and couldn't sleep and couldn't stand being sober or awake or alone, and all that engaged me was compulsively calling my ex-husband—the therapist at the college counseling center drew up a contract stipulating that I would not call my ex for a week and then two weeks and then three. This worked and I want to do it again but Paula pushes for something deeper. She will not play TRIAGE NURSE.

I go home and research my symptoms online. Google matches CUTTING and MOTHER and ADDICT and RELATIONSHIPS and comes up with a diagnosis in minutes.

BORDERLINE PERSONALITY DISORDER.

Shit. THOSE PEOPLE ARE CRAZY.

I had heard of borderline personality disorder when I worked in the university counseling office as an undergraduate English tutor. A woman walked in one day, a streak of dark hair and an open black raincoat. She asked to see one of the graduate-student counselors. No one would tell her anything. Everyone just wanted her to leave. When she left the office, the student worker staffing the front desk turned to me and said, "She's a borderline. They'll stalk you." That's the start and finish of what most people know about borderline personality.

As recently as January 2009, *Time* magazine poked and prodded "The Mystery of Borderline Personality Disorder" without revealing much about the lived experience, social history, or psychiatric debates over this slippery mishap of a label. BORDERLINE is a smear of water in the sky, like a metal cup traced in mist along a series of points of light. WOMAN. LESBIAN. HYSTERIC. The words burst into flame like distant stars and died before I was born. Like me they are here and not here. In order to be diagnosed with borderline personality disorder, a person must meet five out of nine criteria.

My eyes widen as they move down the list.
I meet all nine.
Yes I no you do.

DSM IV

CRITERIA FOR
BORDERLINE PERSONALITY DISORDER

A pervasive pattern of instability of interpersonal relationships, self-image, and affects, and marked impulsivity beginning by early adulthood and present in a variety of contexts, as indicated by five (or more) of the following:

1. Frantic efforts to avoid real or imagined abandonment. NOTE: Do not include suicidal or self-mutilating behavior covered in Criterion 5.

2. A pattern of unstable and intense interpersonal relationships characterized by alternating between extremes of idealization and devaluation.

3. Identity disturbance: markedly and persistently unstable self-image or sense of self.

4. Impulsivity in at least two areas that are potentially self-damaging (e.g., spending, sex, substance abuse, reckless driving, binge eating). NOTE: Do not include suicidal or self-mutilating behavior covered in Criterion 5.

5. Recurrent suicidal behavior, gestures, or threats, or self-mutilating behavior.

6. Affective instability due to a marked reactivity of mood (e.g., intense episodic dysphoria, irritability, or anxiety usually lasting a few hours and only rarely more than a few days.

7. Chronic feelings of emptiness.

8. Inappropriate, intense anger or difficulty controlling anger (e.g., frequent displays of temper, constant anger, recurrent physical fights).

9. Transient, stress-related paranoid ideation or severe dissociative symptoms.

———

"I don't know how much you know about the DSM." My therapist walks this question backwards towards me. I scan the stack of books on the chair beside Paula's desk and recognize a few titles.

"Some."

"Do you know about Axis I and Axis II disorders?"

"No." I listen to her describing Axis I, where mood disorders like depression and anxiety are grouped, and Axis II, where more deeply entrenched conditions appear.

I wait for her to tell me I have the less serious one. But she doesn't.

This is when I start to worry.

I flash on a memory of a sculpture I saw in Paris the summer I was twenty. I was museum hopping to distract myself from the anxiety of not being able to reach my husband by phone for weeks. *Where could he be? What's going on?* I called my grandmother and asked her to tell him to call me. I ate almost nothing. I walked and walked and walked. I said angry things about French people and ate McDonald's in protest of my exile. I wrote fake-happy notes on postcards with pictures of the *Arc de Triomphe* and sent them to my sisters. I ate peanut butter and listened to Enya on the train to Nimes and spoke to no one. I called our apartment in Georgia at all hours of the day and night hoping the lack of communication was a fluke of transatlantic separation and not something more serious. Like divorce. Moths ate the inner lining of my stomach while I wandered through museums of work by Pablo Picasso and Auguste Rodin.

That's when I saw her. A woman made of stone.
And fell instantly in love.

Camille Claudel was a sculptor but sometimes she took her clothes off and modeled postures of despair, anguish, and exhaustion for her married artist boyfriend. I imagine her crouching on the bare wooden floor of his atelier with her arms held tight around her torso in the naked loneliness of self-soothing. The body flexed to the point of pain produces the most compelling planes and twists. I read somewhere that Rodin preferred his models to be hurting physically while he worked their forms in pencil or stone. Beyond the call of art, his capacity to witness a woman's misery without intervening served him well in his personal life. He was sleeping with Camille but would not leave his wife, Rose, for her. Camille and Rose put up with the long insult for fifteen years, until Auguste made the mistake of forcing Camille to have an abortion. When he had his fetus removed from the house of her body, she decided he wasn't the greatest catch after all. Seven years later she was still thinking about him, worrying her former lover wanted to kill her. People said she was deranged. She barricaded herself in her cottage and broke her best statues and then an asylum ate her whole.

"Systematic persecution delirium," the doctors called it.

"Mostly based upon false interpretations and imagination."

Fifteen years past Camille's faux diagnosis her friend-girl Jessie tried to spring her belatedly from the bin. The doctors probably thought Camille was not ARTIST but LESBIAN so they didn't listen. Camille Claudel crouched in the belly of the wail for thirty years before her limbs reached the rigor mortis peak of hard perfection. The woman who sculpted as if her hands were on fire forgot what stone looked like but remembered exactly how it feels.

Signs in the *Musèe Rodin* instruct visitors not to touch the women but my fingertips ached for them. I walked in the garden outside the museum, beneath an arch called *The Gates of Hell* carved with images from Greek mythology of women paying dearly for mistakes they called love or loyalty. When Paula tells me I have borderline personality disorder I smile calmly and make my mouth say a picture perfect *thank you* like a curtsy. My real self crouches on the floor with clouds in her eyes. My head throbs with an endless row of women pouring water into clay jugs that never fill up.

THERAPISTS ARE CAUTIOUS in planning the moment of diagnosis. If it happens too soon, the label may have a splintering effect on the person. She may act out. She may resist. She may say THIS IS BULLSHIT. She may say YOU'RE FULL OF IT. She may embrace the diagnosis as an excuse and become sicker than ever. I open my mouth and without wincing let Paula spoon the bitter word onto my tongue. I smile and say thank you. I know I'm not childish like other patients. I know I'm strong. I know I can handle it. I have grace under pressure. Good character. I know how to face the truth and do what's best and work on myself to become well.

I am

1. DOCILE BODY
2. GOOD GIRL
3. DEAN'S LIST
4. ROCKET SCIENTIST
5. SECRET FAVORITE

IF IT KILLS ME.

I make up for being borderline by reading fat books with hard words. I want to understand everything about borderline personality disorder. I want to be the best borderline personality ever. I want to be AMAZING.

THE BORDERLINE DOES NOT ACCEPT HER OWN INTELLIGENCE, ATTRACTIVENESS, OR SENSITIVITY AS CONSTANT TRAITS, BUT RATHER AS COMPARATIVE QUALITIES TO BE CONTINUALLY RE-EARNED AND JUDGED AGAINST OTHERS. FOR THE BORDERLINE, IDENTITY IS GRADED ON A CURVE. WHO SHE IS AND WHAT SHE DOES TODAY DETERMINES HER WORTH, WITH LITTLE REGARD TO WHAT HAS COME BEFORE. THE BORDERLINE ALLOWS HERSELF NO LAURELS ON WHICH TO REST. LIKE SISYPHUS, SHE IS DOOMED TO ROLL THE BOULDER REPEATEDLY UP THE HILL, NEEDING TO PROVE HERSELF OVER AND OVER AGAIN.

—JEROLD KREISMAN AND HAL STRAUS,
I Hate You, Don't Leave Me:
Understanding the Borderline Personality

I play psychologist—sitting on my couch explaining myself and our affair to Emily—diverting myself from the work of separating from her and striving towards my own psychological integration. I read like someone is handing out gold stars. I immerse myself in the diagnosis like warm water specked with Epsom salts. The diagnosis becomes another way to make her love me.

Just look at all this WORK! All this KNOWLEDGE!

Emily and I move carefully through December, sharing birthday cupcakes and Christmas gifts and phone conversations while I get used to my new self-image and invite Emily to resume her role as GOOD BREAST. I am the BAD OBJECT. I am the site of shame. I take full responsibility for the problems between Emily and me even though Paula insists our relationship would drive anyone crazy. I can't hear this yet.

It's simpler if it's all me.
Then it's in my hands to fix.

I read above my grade level, laboring through Marsha Linehan and using terms like INVALIDATING ENVIRONMENT and EMOTIONAL DYS-REGULATION that feel noble on my tongue. I connect the dots between my romantic obsession—*pick me! pick me!*—and my workaholism and see how my terror of being discarded by Emily is joined at the root with my terror of the tenure process with its rigorous annual reviews. I practice saying *I am emotionally dysregulated right now* to myself when I feel anxious. The naming calms me. DYSREGULATION sounds like the timing in a car—something that can be fixed with a quick tune-up and a new hose or two. I spread notes like roadmaps on my dining room table. Each theory loosens the obsession a little more. Each typology helps tell me why I can't shake it. I bury myself in them. Pull them on top of me the way people with autism crawl under mattresses. Calmed by the steady pressure.

I try on the lens of borderline personality disorder and watch my romantic history snap into focus. The way I couldn't break up with my high school boyfriend even though I hated him. Even though he broke my nose, took me to McDonald's to wash the blood from my face and hands, leaned towards my ear during English the next day and told me I would grow old and die alone.

We screamed at each other in cars and hallways.
I played sad music when we broke up and drove from one end of town to the other looking for him.
nothing compares 2 u

I became resigned to a future I did not want.

I would have to marry him because I depended on him in ways I didn't understand and couldn't change.

I interrupted the flow of destiny by marrying someone else and choosing a whole other future I did not want, the one where my husband leaves me while I study elegant shapes of loss before returning home to perform a manic ballet of failed mourning. I almost didn't graduate from college on schedule because I stopped going to class, but then the threat of public shame jolted me into action to disguise the facts of entropy and dysregulation. I begged for extensions and completed the work of spring quarter in three weeks. I didn't want anyone to know I let grief throw me off my game.

My diagnosis meets with the same defensive fervor.

I want to do borderline personality the BENJAMIN FRANKLIN WAY. *Self-reliant.* A loaf of bread under each arm and optimism in my heart as I rise above my meek beginnings. This is the bargaining stage of grief. I attempt to cancel out inner badness by increasing intellectual productivity. NO MORE TAVERNS, GAMES, OR FROLICS. I imagine myself telling Oprah how I hit rock bottom and then turned it all around.

Early to bed, early to rise, makes a borderline healthy, wealthy, and wise.

I want to sing the borderline electric. I want the buzz and hum of words in my mouth. I want to be facing the other way when the moment of impact finally comes.

Do I contradict myself? VERY WELL THEN, I CONTRADICT MYSELF.

WE BORDERLINES CONTAIN MULTITUDES.

ALICE MILLER DOESN'T get a fair shake in the world of psychology.

She is anti-spanking. She is intense. She is in places overbearing. Her renunciation of membership from the International Psychoanalytic Association may have been a schizotypal reaction with histrionic features. Point granted. But I say take what you like and leave the rest, and I like Alice Miller for intervening in the usual suppression of concern for hurt feelings. She says human beings have needs. We come into the world expressing them from our first thin squeal after sliding from our mother's bodies in a rude flood. All too soon we are toiling away at the impossible work of accommodating the needs of the people around us—"spoken and unspoken, reasonable and unreasonable"—and we get mixed up. We stop looking to our emotions for direction. They are too often in conflict with the expectations of our environment and the people who have real pull, real juice.

Alice Miller says *hold up / wait a minute / let me put some boom in it*. Needs are *not* foolish or too much.

They do not need to be suppressed or apologized for. WE ARE NOT MADE OF STEEL. We have needs! Okay?! And parents and lovers and friends are supposed to listen and respond appropriately. If they can't—Alice Miller says *when* they can't—the CHILD WIFE LOVER loses a piece of her humanity. We chip each other's fragile edges and step away from the mess as if we are not responsible. Deal or no deal. Pact or no pact.

This doesn't seem to bother Emily.

She stays in her own psychological space because she's a BITCH just like Maureen.

> *This is me mad, not my most attractive side, a mean*
> *dark rut I get stuck in sometimes. My voice is*
> *unfamiliar. My smallest person comes out. I call*
> *people names and point out flaws like I'm wearing*
> *glitter and ostrich and storming the stage as a rising*
> *legend—Lisa Labeija, former protégé of Linda*
> *Extravaganza of the House of Extravaganza—*
> *specializing in the ancient art of the verbal ninja.*

THE PSYCHIATRIST LAWRENCE KAYTON published an article in the *Journal of Youth and Adolescence* in December 1972—the same month I squirmed from the birth canal into the lurid lights of a Christmas tree—on vampires and the phenomenology of schizophrenics. Both respond to real or perceived deprivation with oral sadism. Bit-ing is the shadow side of sucking. Intimacy hurts. The caped embrace cloaks the attack.

THE HEART EXISTS TO BE STOLEN, DRAINED, SPIT-ROASTED, AND DEVOURED.

Kayton says non-vampires need to cut vampires a break.

Look at the dilemma they face! How about some empathy for the undead? *Imagine opening your mouth and finding attachment hunger so vast the virgin objects of affection run screaming or shrivel in your arms like dried fruit.*

BORDERLINES—whose rage marks a dramatic pit stop on the schizoaffective spectrum—know LOVE BITES. Our rage is perverse. Like a strange child, the rage walks backwards. Sarcasm takes scattered steps in a zigzag towards the beloved. In the most disorganized moments, the borderline throws her whole body sideways in the leap and spin of a parasuicidal gesture, emptying a bottle of Klonopin into her mouth and chewing the chalky yellow pills while her spouse scrapes the paste from her tongue with desperate tooth-nicked fingers.

High-pitched shrieks followed by the sound of air entering a slit throat is borderline for PLEASE STAY. The noise distracts me from the feeling underneath the rage.

The tantrum is a form of panic attack.

The borderline buries the prohibited childhood feelings of rage and sorrow in shallow graves. The decomposing body of half-eaten grief rises up before my waking eyes, worms crawling from its eyes and nose, hunks of flesh torn from the face and neck.

I drive the narrow circle from home to campus to therapy and home again singing angry songs and picturing myself punching the glass of my windshield. I want to watch the barrier crack from the force of my fist, like a cement sidewalk giving way to the wild desperation of dandelions. I want to see my anger as the poetry of a flower etched in glass. I want the delusion of falling apart that looks like a dying swan or a swirl of yellow leaves in the brilliant harvest season.

It would be more accurate to admit the anger is a stone thrown through the antique stained glass windows of a church. The anger is a drunkard singing lewd songs at a funeral. The anger is an addict putting a knife into your liver before taking ten dollars from your wallet for a fix. The anger is bold and destructive and frightening and not at all beautiful. I am having visions of entrails and blood splatter patterns. I am beginning to scare myself.

"I don't want you to take this literally," I say to Paula. I edge slowly into territory that could be interpreted as psychotic. "I don't want you to put me in the hospital for this," I say, and she nods.

"These words keep running through my head like a mantra. They are not words I want to act on, but whenever I feel frustrated or shut out from life with Emily or from life in my department, I think these words over and over." I am stalling.

"What are they?"

"I want to be bloody." I watch her face closely.
"I want to be out of here." I am relieved when she does not look shocked.

"What that sounds like to me is a fantasy of purging."

I picture blood running down my forearms. And then I picture getting the fuck out. Just being gone. This is the only way I know to break free of this wild loop of grief. Or I could kill Emily. My mind flashes on a terrible image of bashing Emily's head in. The logic of the crime of passion fashions my longing for Emily into a lethal weapon. I want to annihilate the source of my frustration.

Funny story. A female astronaut in dark wig and trench coat confronts a woman in an airport parking lot in Orlando for threatening to steal the astronaut's boyfriend. Police discover a steel mallet, a four-inch knife, a BB gun, and a bunch of large trash bags in her trunk.

I don't blink an eye at the details of Lisa Nowak's public breakdown.

Of course she drove fourteen hours straight through the night to meet her love rival at an airport and maybe kill her or maybe scare her. Of course she wore a diaper so she wouldn't have to stop the car. *People* magazine ran the story of this love triangle under the headline OUT OF THIS WORLD, but that's hardly the case and I suspect the people at *People* know this.

One day in tenth grade I pulled a freshman girl out of her English class and asked to see her in the school bathroom. I heard she made a date with my ex-boyfriend. We sat side by side on the tile floor. I stared straight ahead as I warned her quietly that the date was not a good idea. My whole body trembled with anger. One night I left tire marks in her yard to protest the pain of my break up— big wordless arcs of red dirt gashing her grassy lawn—then her mother chased me down and cursed at me in the Wendy's parking lot. I hit her daughter in the face in that same parking lot a week later, chanting at her, "You're so fucking ugly," over and over until she got out of her car to face me. She split my lip and I pulled her hair and then we stopped. I washed my face in the bathroom and went home to bed.

I WANTED TO SEEM CRAZY. MY MOTHER TAUGHT ME THIS.

Make them nervous, she said, *not sure what you might do. People give you elbow room if they think you might not be quite in control of yourself. Roll your eyes side to side. Walk backwards. Don't worry about what they think. Here's what matters. Take what you need.*

Growl like a dog.

Claim the food bowl with your body.

If all else fails, GO FERAL.

My usual sad but stable mood state metamorphoses over time in response to the prolonged intermittent availability of my obsessive target. I slip in and out of secret psychosis like a second skin. The airless cockpit of the mood astronaut feels like home.

3 LEVELS OF EMOTIONAL FUNCTIONING IN BORDERLINE PERSONALITY

1. Depressed, bored, and lonely
2. Angry, controlling, paranoid, and manipulative behaviors in response to anticipated loss of attachment
3. Nihilistic dissociation and raging fights, often fueled by the disinhibiting effects of alcohol or substance abuse

—JOHN GUNDERSON,
Borderline Personality Disorder: A Clinical Guide

By the time Paula proposes borderline personality as a possible diagnosis for me I am fluctuating between levels two and three on John Gunderson's list. I meet the diagnosis like I'd meet a lost friend I never missed, with false cheer and a cascade of excuses. I speak of it in the artificial exuberance used on family vacations and dates that fail to amuse. *Had a great time! Call me tomorrow! Wish you were here! Let's do this again! It's good that you feel this; you tend to intellectualize.*

I want to be the exception to the rule.

I want to be the one borderline personality on the planet who receives this painful and frightening diagnosis and springs into heroic action. I want to pack my diagnosis like I'm packing a studio apartment in a U-Haul full of clearly labeled boxes and relocate to new and exciting psychological frontiers. Borderline personality is my big apple—*If I can make it here, I can make it anywhere! It's up to you!*—I toss my hat into the air like I can take on the world.

I am not exceptional.

Like many people in therapy, I want too much and too little. I want to be better right now. I better be right all the time. I want to skate scot-free. I scoot on my tail when the slope gets too steep. I want the card that says GET OUT OF JAIL FREE. I want to be free to be you and me. I respond to the diagnosis as if rocket fuel is sending me fast into the rough friction of borderline psychopathology. Red zone. Recalcitrant. Ballistic. In the following weeks I conduct the business of borderline personality as *Challenger* space shuttle disaster. I am Christa McAuliffe coming apart in the sky.

TANTRUM ARTIST

Borderline personality disorder is a form of madness made of mood disorders and neurological malfunctions. People with borderline personality heat up fast and have trouble cooling back down. Emotions run high. Impulse and inhibition run together like hot and cold water from a tap. Once the borderline body reaches this place of hypervigilance and despair, every day presents new evidence of apocalypse and new opportunities for hysteria and resignation.

One of my students attempts suicide.

One of my students starts to flirt with me.

In between this riptide of people I care about moving-away and moving-towards, my mind slips and twists and goes haywire. Something inside me crumples. I put my head down on the desk. Students flow around my desk and out the door. I gather my books and notes and go home, thinking about Neal in a coma a few blocks from campus. Two weeks ago he stood in my office and cried without shame over his broken heart.

FIRST GIRLFRIEND. FIRST BREAK UP.

Evan saw me crumple in class. He emails that night. He wants to know if I'm okay. I never understood how professors could find common ground with students, how desire and comfort might assemble in the space between our cynicism and their uncertainty. After managing a case of walking melancholia for more than a year, my balance and direction falter and I find myself chasing the moon in a strange boy's eyes. I stand naked in a public square and BARK AGAINST THE DOG STAR.

We are in this together, I think.
The grown-ups don't understand.

He calls and I feel fourteen and giddy inside. We talk about Neal, about regret, about what I could have said or done. He tells me not to feel guilty. He tells me I am GOOD and REAL and ALIVE and VELVET.

I drift off to sleep already high. I flirted back and it should scare me but it doesn't. I don't know who I am, doing this thing I purse my lips at other people for doing.

We go to the Black Box on campus and see a play called *Crave* by Sarah Kane. She was a British playwright who battled bipolar disorder for years before killing herself at twenty-eight. I hear a young actor's voice fill the space with words that will echo in my mind for months:

> The only thing I want to say I've said already, and it's a bit fucking tedious to say it again, no matter how true it is, no matter that it's the one unifying thought humanity has. HOW CAN YOU LEAVE ME LIKE THIS?

I will step to their cadence across campus and around the block each evening as I walk my dogs in the sandy margins of the roads in my neighborhood.

Evan and I go to a bar and start out on opposite sides of the table but our conversation grows so intense it pulls me from one side of the table to the other. We talk fiercely with each other, heads together and hands animated. We drink whiskey in plastic cups. I tell him he is a flower that BLOSSOMED IN A MUD PUDDLE. It's a line about a girl from a novella I'm teaching. He says that's the coolest thing anyone ever said about him. We talk and talk and talk. Evan tells me he was recently diagnosed with bipolar disorder. I tell him I have borderline personality disorder. I open up about myself, about my chronic depression, about my divorce when I was twenty, about the relentlessness of loneliness and the alienation of always having to seem okay.

He hints at problems in his relationship.

Yes! He has a girlfriend too.

He talks about sometimes becoming so frustrated he punches the wall in the bathroom where he works, about his therapist and his new meds, about the ways Neal's suicide attempt keeps hitting him in random spurts and waves, and finally about the way we can maybe LAME, POETIC, ROMANTIC, HE ADMITS IT heal each other. About how maybe the wounds of two people can somehow mend together.

We grin. OUR BROKEN PARTS MATCH.

I say *I hope it doesn't look weird that we're talking to each other so much.*

He says *Fuck you we're saving each other's lives* to our imagined critics.

Yes. That is what we are doing. I feel dazed by his intensity. We hug twice in the parking lot. Rush home to email each other. We email each other twenty times a day. I don't feel so alone anymore.

He tells me he needs this.

He tells me he hopes I need it too.

And I do.

AFTER SITTING IN the hospital parking lot crying myself hoarse, I need him to make me feel better. I need him like a new addict needs a twenty bag of heroin.

For pleasure, partly, but mostly to stop the pain.

After fifteen months of wearing down my sanity locked in a love triangle with Emily and her partner, I have given up all semblance of doing the right thing. I start signing my emails *Love, Lisa* and he starts signing his messages *love evan. Not trying to be a copycat,* he explains, *just trying to say yes i get it too.*

This is when things start to heat up.

We stand with our thumbs in our back pockets, the sound of tennis shoes shifting on asphalt filling the silences in our conversation. I ask if he wants to get a drink or sit in the car and talk. He chooses SIT IN THE CAR AND TALK, and I find a remote parking lot on campus, turn the music up, lean across the front seat and put my mouth on his.

The disk plays and plays.

The final track starts, a cover of "Against All Odds" by The Postal Service. I have been raised on the sadness of this song. My mother listened to the original Phil Collins version when my father left her. I sat in the backseat of the car memorizing the words "You're the only one who really knew me at all," thinking, *She doesn't feel that way.* Thinking, *She's just mad, she's just embarrassed.*

I laugh and tell Evan I already feel sad when I hear this song, like I'm walking around with a prepackaged kit of emotions ready to unwrap when the end comes.

"I have fast-forwarded to the end of our relationship," I tell him, "already pictured the moment when I will want to say to you, 'How can I just let you walk away?' When I will want to say, 'Turn around and see me cry.'"

I think he will find this as amusing as I do. *I am an empty space,* har har.

Instead he winces, cuts his eyes sideways. "Why would you do that?"

———

If you look up the phrase INAPPROPRIATE LOVE OBJECT in the dictionary, you will see Evan's picture there.

The details float in my mind like buoys warning swimmers not to go farther out.

> Evan is my student.
>
> Evan is twenty-one.
>
> Evan has a live-in girlfriend.
>
> Evan is in treatment for bipolar disorder.
>
> Evan is moving to Michigan.

I take a deep breath and swim past each one
like a child pulling off her life preserver in the
roiling ocean waters.

The absurdity of my fixation on Evan is what finally helps me—several months after the diagnosis of borderline personality disorder—recognize my obsessions as a pattern, as something that goes on inside me. It is also the moment when the people around me recognize I have a disorder, where before they just thought I was getting a raw deal from Emily. They watch in horror as I transfer the balance of my emotional account from one attachment fetish person to another.

The crush on Evan would most likely have stayed on the level of compulsive email and the occasional stolen kiss except for what happens next, which takes me by surprise and changes the infatuation into something more real and less comfortable, something more physical and less fun. Kat invites Evan and Nicholas to join us for an academic conference on popular culture in Atlanta, and I know instantly that this is not a good idea but when Evan calls to ask if I want to cancel my plane reservation, ride to Atlanta with him, I say yes.

THIS IS NOT A GOOD IDEA. I SAY YES.

This contradiction encapsulates everything I know about my relationship history.

We moon and argue and drink too much and nurse hangovers together while we're in Atlanta. He gives me a toe massage at the dinner table on a patio. I love his reaction to my statement that my toe hurts. No invalidation. No melodrama. Just responsiveness. Precisely what is missing in my emotional life with Emily.

"No matter what happens with us, don't go back to her, okay? You deserve more." I nod in agreement.

ON THE INTERSTATE home from Atlanta, Evan stops talking about breaking up with Leanne and starts talking about feeling guilty.

When I hear the words *I feel guilty* my insides go hot.

I look at him in disbelief. Like I don't know who he is. Like I could not see this coming. I want to stick a pin in him to wake him up. I want to slap him like they slap hysterical women in movies. I fold left arm over right, dig four fingernails into the flesh facing out the passenger side window.

"I'm sorry," he says when we get home. "I want to be with you. I just can't. I can't do this to Leanne. This isn't the right time. I can't do this. I want to. I can't."

I stare out the window of the back door. I try to keep my mouth closed but I hiss and sputter and spill over. I am whispering through the dirt in my mouth.

I am BLOODROOT MORPHINE FEVER PRAYER.

I put my head on the kitchen counter and let tears and saliva pool under my face. My crazy parts are showing and I don't care.

I can't go through this again.
I CAN'T GO THROUGH THIS AGAIN.
I CAN'T GO THROUGH THIS AGAIN.
I CAN'T GO THROUGH THIS AGAIN.
I CAN'T GO THROUGH THIS AGAIN.

He tucks me into bed, takes my swollen face in his hands, and tongues salt from the insides of my mouth. I tell him I don't want him to go. My face is cradled against his chest. I breathe in the scent of his body through his *please don't eat birds* T-shirt. When he leaves I feel as if I've been locked out of my house and can't get back in.

I take a blade from my bedside table drawer

and set it down beside me.

I call Emily at work.

Tell her I need help.

She comes over and listens as I spill everything. The student. The obsession. The panic. She reassures me that my indiscretion is not life-and-death bad, not lose-your-job-if-you-get-found-out bad. We spend the day together, drinking small glasses of whiskey and melting back in love.

She tells me things I don't know how to absorb.

She loves me more than ever. She kissed another one of our coworkers just weeks before she kissed me. It was a man. Lyle. *I knew it!* I wasn't the first one she cheated with. I am stunned by this discovery.

"But you *were* the first one," she insists. "The first woman. The only one who mattered."

I am cut to my core by the image of her with this man, whom I had seen flirting with her in the hallways for months. I feel betrayed and misled. We keep talking, trying to get somewhere, but by nine o'clock that night, she has to go home.

"I have a child," she reminds me.

And a partner, I think but don't say.

I make the pain go away by deciding I don't want her to stay. I go in my bedroom and lock the door.

"Just get out!" Teeth bared, fists clinched.

> She leaves and I rock back and forth
> with the razor blade in my hand.

I sit and cry and rock like I am rocking a baby in my lap. She is inconsolable. I want to put the crying in a car and watch it roll into a lake. I push the blade back and forth across the thin skin of my wrist. I make one cut, then another right next to it, then another, each time thinking *just one more,* but I don't stop. I line them up tightly, a series of straight red wounds about two inches long covering my forearm from wrist to inner elbow. It's not enough. I move the blade diagonally across the ones closest to my wrist, carving a section of delicate cross-hatchings that trail off at the curve of my arm, then push on around to the more visible outer side.

Yes, I think, *Do it.*
GIVE IN.
GO CRAZY.
I am not afraid.

I have taken a dose of Xanax prescribed for stage fright. Instead of making me relax and fall asleep it puts me in a trance. Books on pharmaceutical treatments for borderline personality blacklist Xanax. It reduces panic as we walk along the narrow canyon rim of self-annihilation. We stare with stone eyes at our open skin.

I'm speaking in first person plural now. WE.
My voice sometimes splits into three parts.

The boy I miss is someone I barely know. A PLACEHOLDER and STUNT DOUBLE. Our fast affair is an arena for tenderizing old twists of emotion, to make them pliable enough to pass from my body. Until now they hung forgotten from the rafters of my psyche, drying into tough strips. Inedible bits of meat bereft of nutrients and hard as tree bark. They mark my intestines with fissures and clog my elimination system. Instead of getting the old feelings out I strain my abdomen and pass nothing but blood. The tantrum of loving a sweet lost boy and then losing him is triggered by a mass of displaced rage and guilt and shame about a childhood crime I committed but was never convicted of.

> TANTRUM BEHAVIOR CAN BE TRACED BACK
> TO CHILDHOOD RELATIONSHIPS WHERE AFFECTION
> WAS NEVER FREE OF CONFLICTFUL FEELING.
> —THEODORE MILLON,
> *Personality Disorders in Modern Life*

I was eleven years old. I ABANDONED MY SISTERS.

I trained myself to say it was okay. It was not okay. I became my own untrustworthy narrator. I told myself lies. I hid secrets like green peas in air pockets in my lungs and hoped my lungs would not stop breathing. I knew things I didn't want to know. I didn't want to know I was not okay. I didn't want to know I was a liar.

I learned loss. ORPHAN. AMPUTEE. LONE WOLF from a PACK OF THREE.

I lost the closeness of nightly baths and shared neglect and small comforts like the rough texture of clean terry cloth stretched across Melissa's stomach under my palm. Melissa hardly knew me the first time we saw each other after I moved in with our father. She was two. I reached for her and she pulled back. Something broke inside me. I rode with my father to pick up my sisters every other weekend but it was all surface and show and frustration. We were no longer sisters in the same way. We were no longer the same people. Because I lived with emotion-phobic minimizers, my attachment loss was explained away, like clouds on a day when you plan to go swimming. It was dressed up in holiday finerie. It was put on a back shelf and marked as POISON. The shelf was never secure and now it caves inside me.

Something strong is pouring out on the floor.
My sisters need me and I can't help them.

The pain is almost more than I can bear. All of us are grown women now—thirty-seven, thirty-one, and twenty-eight—and we live the chaos of attachment gone awry.

Second daughter in the birth order and six years younger than I am, JESSICA structured her life around impossible security. She loved women who wouldn't love her back. Selfish women. Cruel women. Women with no interest in becoming better people. She understood love as asymmetrical and self-destructive. Picture her riding away in a police car after trying to help her girlfriend run away from the cops. Picture her slamming the door on her arm again and again until a purple and green bouquet blooms on her skin. Picture her closed up in her house taking this drug and that drug, then convulsing on the floor and calling out for death until she went silent in cardiac arrest. Jessica waded through waist-deep bogs of depression without treatment during adolescence and adulthood. She hated her body. She hated her little sister. She hated a world that wrote her off for being awkward but offered no tools she could use to become amazing. In the dark living room of the same house where she grew up, she self-medicated with benzos and cable and self-injurious behaviors like clipping her nails off from cuticle to tip. She removed them like she was setting something free, fingers like birds suffocating beneath slicks of keratin. She could not breathe. Even her skin suffocated, like a plastic bag in the windpipe. She had to get it off. For ten years—ages fourteen to twenty-five—she pared skin from her hands like she was peeling mangos, turning her palms into hot pink flares and fake-praying no one would notice.

And guess what?

Her wicked wish comes true like cherry pie. Easy.

Our mother never sews anymore but in a one-in-a-million chance of immaculate mutilation she pricks her finger on a broken spindle she finds in the folds of her rose-covered comforter. The whole family falls asleep—all of them—far and wide. Mother, sister, father, and cat fall asleep. Stepmonster #1, stepmonster #2 both hear the alarm and both hit snooze. Cousins catnap five counties over. Her imaginary friend yawns like a girl who just wants to spoon but Jessica is too distracted for kisses so the pretend friend flounces towards the door. *This is silly I'm leaving.* Jessica tromps and snorts from one end of the Cracker Jack box to the other and decides to bunker down in the bathroom. The tub smokes and boils like her blood.

SHE WANTS TO BURN.

She wants more than 50 percent.

When her skin melts and twists she says *Good you deserve it bitch.*

She holds the waxy sign of her scars beneath the surface and watches the words SAVE OUR SHIP break apart like old blisters. The rule of thumb in her mental asylum is NO HOLDS BARRED. *Jessica is her own prisoner of war and Geneva Conventions do not apply.* Water fills the cavities of her face to simulate the sensation of drowning while the interrogation drones on and on. She breaks down. Cries uncle. Offers up her virgin sister. Sharpened tips of wild bamboo grow towards her naked chest.

The door to the bathroom remains locked.

Our parents lick sugarplums from their lips in their sleep.

MY MOTHER DOES NOT do single well. She needs a man like a superego to cork the bottle and put her to bed. Beyond the eyes of Big Brother, she is all bulimia and bad credit. She hoards and gorges like an orphan. The feeling of NO ONE IS LOOKING leaves her wild-eyed and dazed by freedom. Jessica and Melissa grew up in one of the worst periods of Mother's life. The eighties—era of neon shoelaces and matching plastic earrings. Right around the time Harry met Sally our mother's casual neglect crossed into criminal negligence. She ate Somas like Alka-Seltzers and slurred her words so BRATS sounded like BRISS or BATS. She passed out on the kitchen floor while cube steak popped and sighed on the stove. My sisters thought she was mentally retarded.

They laughed and pointed.

Mother became crippled from rheumatoid arthritis in her thirties and the diagnosis pleased her. It meant legitimate grounds for requesting more narcotics from her doctor. By the time I reached my twenties, she was ingesting a hundred pain pills a week. Minimum.

She almost let the house burn down around their ears.

She almost lost my sisters to the state.

Both sisters developed deformed coping mechanisms for the boredom and self-loathing that comes from being parented by an addict.

My youngest sister MELISSA bears the grotesque beauty of a splatter film. Bright colors. Sudden terrors. A blonde heroine always losing her head, she moves through the world spurting blood from the open mouth of her jagged neck. She walks through walls and speedballs with zombies on the other side. Her life is a piece of foreboding music in a minor key. Here is what makes this story sad. Melissa was born applejack sunbeam pure, hair like a platinum halo, smiling like a Gerber baby at a photo shoot. She was two the day I put her in a crib and followed my father out the door forever. Twenty-five years later she still spits fire at our feet. Her life is a wrecked boat torn apart for kindling and set ablaze to send a message to the sky from a deserted beach.

From a distance the words spell SAVE ME.

The closer the sign the clearer the statement.
Turns out it says, FUCK YOU.

At twelve Melissa had not yet turned strange. The corner from twelve to thirteen cut sharply to the side into an alley marked one-way. She changed homes. She changed schools. She changed rules. She changed friends. She kissed boys with bad teeth and racks in their trucks for shotguns. She sidled up to manic girls with mothers who were maids and shared cigarettes with thirteen-year-olds like best friends. Melissa wanted to be a mother like that. Young and cool and devil-may-care. She wanted to be a mother with kids who liked her. She believed popularity required her to pop out her puppies while still of eligible age for homecoming queen. She imagined trailing toddlers who would play entourage to her starlet. She had sex without condoms and prayed Jesus would make her pregnant. She is a sexual stunt driver more for dare than pleasure and prides herself on having no boundaries in the area of intercourse.

"I give them whatever they want," she says.

She skipped NYMPHET and went straight for NYMPHO—AC/DC from day one.

She picks sex partners like some people rescue cats. Boys with no front teeth and their best skinny friends. Obese girls. Angry misfits mud-riding in the middle of the night, hooting and yipping at fantasies of parents shot in the face by escaped crazies from Bartow County corrections. She dated the same boy from fourteen to eighteen, when she could finally legally marry him, but she left him a year later because he played video games and smoked pot and shot blanks. Before she asked for divorce she met a dapper con man with a silver tongue and a business plan to get rich selling crank. He took her investment of a thousand dollars and promised a profit of 200 percent. Instead he passed plastic bags of powder and rocks to all the peasants of the land.

Jessica yelled at Melissa to WAKE UP AND SMELL THE CRACK ROCK. The con man was a liar and a thief throwing a party in her house where people snorted profits for breakfast. Melissa nodded her head and agreed to put the bad man out of her life forever. When Jessica woke up, Melissa was gone like Sunday morning. Melissa's husband went home, threw her things out the door, and set them on fire in the yard. Melissa stayed gone for months. She came back pregnant with the con man's son.

We held a white wedding in her ninth month.

Melissa's second husband was equal parts methhead and fake minister. He said the blessing when the family gathered for holiday dinners. He took Melissa to a Church of God and taught her to speak in tongues. The Holy Spirit came out of her mouth like a hot rail. My mother worried the newlyweds would crush her skull with a stone one day to steal the stockpile of Tylox from her storage closet.

Melissa came into the world with a SORCERER'S SKILLS. She waves a wand and sings a song and makes you see what you want to believe. She is exactly who you wish her to be. When she appears to me, Melissa takes the form of a writer. Ten years ago she gave me a book of poetry called *Oedipal Dreams,* by Evelyn Lau, a girl who ran away from home and first published poems at twelve, spunky like a Chinese-Canadian Melissa. At fourteen Lau ran away from home to become things her family would not like.

ANARCHIST. PROSTITUTE. BULIMIC. VAGRANT.

Her titles provoke and harass.

You Are Not Who You Seem. Choose Me. Other Woman.

They could be titles for Melissa's life story. Or my own. The cover art of *Oedipal Dreams* hits you like a cold splash of water. A ghost-white face with two lips like pockets of blood ready to burst. When Melissa loaned me *Oedipal Dreams* I flipped through the pages to see if she had marked anything. I found a corner flipped down on a poem titled "Father." Between our parents, our father was labeled the nicer one because he was more naturally nurturing than our mother, but after he and I split he became to the other sisters something more complex.

Intermittent refuge. Paradise out of reach. Mirage. TAUNT.

AS THE YEARS dragged on and the girls got bitter, they saw the worst in him. ABANDONER. REFUSER. *First-daughter favorer.* He became their story of what might have been. Their lives were love poems to him *Take us with you* and his taillights in their driveway answered in the slam poetry of NO.

For my sisters, our father is the parent who hurt them. They feel as nervous about standing near him as I do about standing near our mother. Easy to villainize the one you don't live with. The other parent becomes the bad object, a convenient storage unit for boxes of reasons why we are the way we are. They remove the pressure to examine the parent who raises us, distracting us too from examining our own compulsions to stage reenactments of emotional trauma. Melissa's feelings about our father, who left before she spoke in full sentences, remain unshaped by words but they come to me through Evelyn Lau in poems I wish Melissa had written.

> you stand cold as a vision
>
> you leave me
>
> I push you through glass doors in my dreams
>
> through skylights
>
> my father with the dark face, you appear more
>
> handsome
>
> in dreams than in life, I hold up to you the handle
>
> of a child's mirror

Lau's poems are slivers and sores and spent bullets. A landscape of needles, broken glass, open flesh, ashes, and amitriptyline, an atmosphere resembling the set of a movie Jessica once loaned me, featuring characters desperate for love, settling for heroin. I recognize this world my sisters paint on the walls around them. I have a history of seeking out music and films and novels that allow me to work from a distance with the dynamics of my own unclaimed hurting.

DOESN'T TAKE MUCH
TO RIP US INTO PIECES, I sang every day for a year.

If Melissa were a book of poems, her back cover would say the same thing Lau's book says. "These are raw, angry poems." I can see the words inscribed across her shoulder blades in gothic letters as if she's a girl in a street gang.

Melissa is a raw angry poem.

The poem says TAKE A GOOD LOOK AT ME NOW.

The poem says HOW CAN I JUST LET YOU WALK AWAY? LET YOU LEAVE WITHOUT A TRACE?

Sweet like syrup of ipecac, she leaves my system with my guts in her hands.

———————

She wants me to know how it feels to be weak and empty. I wish Melissa had become a defiant punk rock street girl poet like Evelyn Lau with an instinct for self-preservation and a notebook full of rage. Instead she dropped acid. She dropped high school. She dropped her sharp poet mind like a bad habit. She dropped out of touch for years, reappearing occasionally as a hysterical phone call or fifteen urgent text messages sent in the middle of the night while I slept. My great-grandfather used to say my spine would grow crooked from holding Melissa on my hip when I was ten and my bones were still hardening in my body. He was right. I think of my scoliosis as a physical mark of lost but not forgotten intimacy with Melissa. I bear the weight in the S-shape of my backbone and carry the memory of my first child like a fist clenched tight around my middle. No one leaves without a trace.

"TO LIVE A LIFE analogous to a soap opera is to live the life of a borderline personality," says psychologist Theodore Millon. The soap opera makes some people dislike us—we are BIRDDOGS, BULLIES, BULLSHITTERS, BAD CHARACTERS—but the soap opera is a symptom. Fireworks splatter across the sky. People in the audience look up at the bright spectacle and can't believe their eyes.

There are reasons for emotional dysregulation.

There are reasons for drinking and cutting, for smoking meth and lighting fires. There is a story that makes sense of all this. Nerve damage and nightmare and nostalgia. A tiny kernel beneath twelve layers of down.

The borderline digs with razor blades, glass slivers, toenail clippers, her own rough nails. Even she is hard pressed to put a finger on it.

BORDERLINES CREATE THE VICIOUS CIRCLES
THEY FEAR MOST. THEY BECOME ANGRY AND DRIVE
THE RELATIONSHIP TO THE BREAKING POINT,
THEN SWITCH TO A POSTURE OF HELPLESSNESS
AND CONTRITION, BEG FOR RECONCILIATION.
IF BOTH PARTIES ARE EQUALLY ENMESHED,
CHAOS AND CONFLICT BECOME THE
SOUL OF THE RELATIONSHIP.
—THEODORE MILLON,
Personality Disorders in Modern Life

———

At the time of the first cut back in December—Emily's initials on the bone-thin skin of my ankle—I think I am the only one going crazy, the only woman over thirty marking up her skin with desperate words like *I love you, I need you* in a warped daisy chain across the top of her foot. I have no idea I am not alone. I have no idea about the company I'm in. All my favorite writers are cutting themselves. All my favorite students are cutting themselves. A man I will sleep with six months from this night is carving the Chinese symbol for NO into his thigh with a knife. *The Chronicle of Higher Education* will call self-cutting a college epidemic. People will make documentaries about it.

MY FAVORITE CELEBRITY DOUBLE Lisa Lopes was not just a pyromaniac. She was also a cutter. She sat in her room at Charter Peachford hospital in Atlanta, mind spinning from the fight and the fire and the aftermath of alcohol abuse treatment. She carved the word LOVE in her forearm from elbow to wrist and later obscured it with its twin emotion—HATE—the letters wider and pushed deeper into the skin. Strong feelings came to her as texts on the body that could only be read one at a time. Scholars call these neurotic mutilations ORGANIC REACTIONS TO PATHOLOGICAL LEVELS OF TENSION AND ANXIETY.

This is the "pride in the power of self-destruction" that psychologist Otto Kernberg writes about in *Borderline Conditions and Pathological Narcissism.* It is the RADICAL FREEDOM of refusing self-preservation and instead bringing blade to skin. It is about the relaxing of vigilance, like taking a harsh drink or a tab of acid. Holding myself rigid with attention to other people's moods and preferences, the relentless effort to win someone over with charm and merits, the ongoing work of building a career and forming a life—all this effort just stops for a minute with the glass of whiskey and razor blade.

The choice to cut is a signal.

I am not trying any more. I am taking a break from doing my best.

The symptom is a window into deep-rooted anxieties, psychotic but not inexplicable. The girl with the broken glass in her hand splits into three parts. She is the parent who hurt her. She is the child who got hurt. She is the parent who failed to protect her. There are reasons why a college professor in her early thirties would sit in her study and slice up her own arm.

> TO EASE TENSION; TO EXPRESS EMOTIONAL PAIN;
> TO PUNISH THE BODY FOR ITS HISTORY OF
> SEXUAL ABUSE, TO ALLEVIATE INNER RAGE,
> TO EXPRESS SHAME, TO PROVIDE BIOCHEMICAL RELIEF.
> —MARILEE STRONG, *A Bright Red Scream*

This last one—biochemical relief—rings truest for me. The cutting is the rebel yell of a body being bombed by implicit memories in the midst of current attachment conflicts.

A storm of emotions.

A tantrum.

Scorched earth.

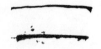

IN EVERYDAY LIFE IT IS POSSIBLE TO OBTAIN
SOME RESPITE FROM MODERATELY HEIGHTENED
LEVELS OF TENSION AND ANXIETY THROUGH
SUCH METHODS AS INCREASED PHYSICAL ACTIVITY,
ORGASM, MEDITATION, AND MUSCLE RELAXATION.
BUT WHEN TENSION AND ANXIETY REACH TRULY
PATHOLOGICAL LEVELS, NONE OF THESE METHODS HAS
MUCH EFFECT. AN ACT OF SELF-MUTILATION, HOWEVER,
MAY BE QUITE EFFICACIOUS IN REDUCING THE TENSION
AND ANXIETY. ONE EXPLANATION FOR THIS EFFECT
RELATES TO THE PROBLEMATIC THEORY OF "PSYCHIC ENERGY."
BRIEFLY STATED, THIS THEORY HOLDS THAT THE MIND-BRAIN
SYSTEM OPERATES BEST WITHIN A CERTAIN RANGE OF
TENSION LEVELS. IF THE LEVEL GETS TOO HIGH,
THE MIND-BRAIN SYSTEM WILL OPERATE AUTOMATICALLY
TO DIVEST ITSELF OF "QUANTITIES OF EXCITATION."
—ARMANDO FAVAZZA, *Bodies Under Seige*

The self-cutting a seizure, the body resets its own buttons.

The cutting is a sign. The anxious adult child of an addict with her codependent can-do spirit screaming, *I cannot do it. I cannot make things work out after all.*

In one of the few memoirs of self-injury, Caroline Kettlewell describes her recovery in terms of neural pathways—the "groove" worn into her mind, the "wrong turns and dark corridors" marked by her history of cutting. Once she learns how to stand "the awful agony of unhappiness" without reverting to the bodily jolt of broken skin, she changes the map of psychological struggle in her mind. "[E]very time I gut it through and survive," she concludes, "I'm reshaping the structure and the chemistry of my thoughts, wearing new paths less tortured and convoluted than the old ones."

Cutting is considered the litmus test of the borderline personality.

If you do it, you are it. Of course being / becoming / defining borderline is not that simple. People cut for other reasons.

Four years from the night I scalp my forearm, a twenty-two-year-old woman named Dominique Fisher in England will be brought up on charges for carving her name into the skin of her lover's arm with a Stanley knife during what newscasters called a drunken fling. They were high on cocaine. They had sex. He tried to steal things from her flat. When she reported him for theft, he countered with the evidence of her text on his body, and then she was the one in trouble. Pre-sentencing reports called her A VERY ISO-

LATED AND NEEDY YOUNG WOMAN. The judge read these words aloud and warned Dominique to cut out the vodka-valium-cocaine cocktails because STRANGE THINGS tend to happen when you get that high. You sway with hypnosis and wax hypergraphic. You carve stars and cross-hatchings and your very long name DOMI-NIQUE into the bare back of your one-night stand.

You ask too much. You risk addiction.
You fill your mouth with figs.
YOU MAY FACE TIME IN JAIL.

The girl scrivener named Dominique Fisher was found guilty of UNLAWFUL WOUNDING. She got served with a suspended sentence, two years of community service, and a stern warning not to take pears from strange goblins.

SUCH STRANGE THINGS MUST NOT HAPPEN AGAIN.

TONIGHT MY MIND is a tornado alley. I scan the June-dark sky. I want the day to stay bright. I want to be higher than high. I want to be peaking all the time. Ella Fitzgerald says spring can really hang you up the most. I picture a noose. I picture my body as strange fruit. Abandonment depression steps to you sudden and mean, and when you have it, spring sounds nothing like the smooth plum silk of a jazz singer's throat. I'm with Jolie Holland on this one. She says springtime can kill you. Jolie lays down the promise of spring renewal like a coiled snake / toothache / a promise your lover wouldn't make and flat dares a girl to pick it back up.

> *Get out of your house before something breaks inside you.*

> *I will leave Emily, leave town, leave this lethal wanting behind soon or else I will die here.*

Eventually I put the blade away and go calmly to bed.
My arm burns all night long like I ran it under scalding water.

I teach class in a sleeveless dress the next day. My face is calm, my smile earnest, the stripes on my arms like exclamation marks punctuating my lecture.

Nice girl. Responsible woman. Nurturing teacher.
The facades break apart.

A madwoman bursts through the seams. I sit at a pub near campus and sip whiskey to kill time before therapy.

BECOMING BORDERLINE
(NOTES ON A FLAWED DIAGNOSTIC LABEL)

THE SHIMMERING, EVER-SHIFTING
BORDERLINE LIKE ALL BOUNDARIES
BECKONS AND ASKS TO BE CROSSED.
—SUSANNAH KAYSEN, *Girl, Interrupted*

"Well, I may or may not be bipolar," I say as I walk into Paula's office. The question of a bipolar II diagnosis had been raised a couple of times in the preceding months. "But I am definitely borderline."

I don't even realize until this moment that I am skeptical of everything Paula says.

Or that I find it hard to believe I have an actual disorder. Much less one that marks me as among the most dreaded of psychoanalytic patients.

BORDERLINE PERSONALITY and BIPOLAR DISORDER may not even be distinct conditions. The questions preoccupying me—about which one I really have, or whether I have both or maybe neither—are psychological defenses. My quest for a term to contain me is not a cure but a clamp. The words hold my broken parts closed so blood doesn't spill on the floor.

Books arrive in the interlibrary loan office and I check them out with zest. How smart the methodical labor of research makes me feel. My immediate fascination with borderline personality is grandiose and self-defeating and does nothing to stop the bleeding. I am a sloppy physician. My sutures barely hold. I leave sponges and scalpels inside. I hold my bare arm out towards Paula as if it says something irrefutable. As if the cuts are stigmata that spontaneously appeared on the surface of my skin to prove borderline dysfunction dwells inside me like a demon. I want her to draw madness from my body and send it running off a cliff in the sallow husks of swine.

"Oh my god. What brought that on?"

Paula busies herself with papers on her desk and asks if it's the worst cutting episode I've ever had.

"Yes," I say.

My eyes sting from sleep deprivation. I wonder if she can tell I've been drinking. "I am pitching a tantrum," I say. I want her to tell me how to stop.

"Are you ready for the hospital?" She is trained to be blunt in confronting my borderline behavior with reminders of consequences. The scars, institutions, the stigma of madness on my permanent record.

"No," I say.

> Secretly I wonder if I really should be locked up.
> If maybe this *is* crazy. If I'm already there and
> just don't know it.

I remember a line from a story about a shipwreck. The moment despair sets in—after several days and nights of battling cold and hunger and thirst and circling sharks—one of the men thinks about giving in and letting himself drown. "Once one is properly wearied," he thinks, "drowning must really be a comfortable arrangement, a cessation of hostilities accompanied by a wave of relief." I think of giving in. I picture nurses and pills and cinderblock walls. I imagine lining up behind the other crazy girls waiting for food and medication and therapy.

> I think of letting myself go under, but I'm not ready.
> "Not yet."

That weekend I go househunting in the new town where I will start over and make myself brand new. Temperatures rise to 80 degrees. I wear long sleeves to hide scabbed cuts on my arm. I go to dinner with a new colleague and when she asks about my life, I am brief and evasive.

I remember that first dinner with Emily when I had just been hired. The drinks. The secrets. My open mouth / open heart / open wounds.

I broke up with Emily. I am getting over Evan.

I can't afford to open up again.

I drive home the next day. For the next six weeks I blur my eyes and time passes like poppies viewed from a fast train. I don't want to feel the ground beneath my feet until I am standing on the other side of the state. I want to walk out on obsession in the early hours while it sleeps. I want to get away from my spoiled identity and the people who watched me fail to thrive. I plan to retrieve my dignity from the waste bin and start over.

Paula tells me to stop being a fool.

"The same predicament awaits you in this new town," she says. "You can't escape your psychology by changing your setting," she says. "You will set up triangles and frustrations and addictions there too. Guaranteed."

BUT LEAVING IS ALL I KNOW TO DO.

WILLIAM FAULKNER WROTE a dramatic fictional account of borderline personality and published it with the title *As I Lay Dying*. The novel is a Gothic Southern love note to a dead woman named Addie Bundren who occupies the empty spaces of emotional refusal. She is not-mother and not-wife. Bitter complaint and cold fish. From the hard bed of her coffin, her body pops and sighs in the heat.

A word is *just a shape to fill a lack,* she says.

Truer words have never been spoken, especially in the academic fields of borderline etiologies, psychopathologies, neuropsychologies, and the gendered social histories of madness, illness, and medicine, where words almost never fit what they are trying to say. Adolph Stern coined the term BORDERLINE PERSONALITY the same decade Faulkner exhumed the details of invalidating environments from the not-grave and not-peace of a woman who believes the purpose of life is to become miserable enough to welcome death with relief. Addie Bundren knows about sound and fury and signifying nothing. She says, *Sin and love and fear are just sounds that people who never sinned nor loved nor feared have for what they never had and cannot have until they forgot the words.*

The same could be said of BORDERLINE PERSONALITY. The syllables may be little more than sounds people make for emotional distress they never felt and won't understand until they drop the word in a lake and walk away.

The psychiatric term BORDERLINE initially described a person whose behavior unfolds between two psychological poles—in the borderlands separating the neurotic from the psychotic. It was based on a very old psychoanalytic paradigm that divided people into treatable (neurotic) and untreatable (psychotic). The need arose for a name to identify people who alternate between periods of disabling anxiety and spirals of angry outbursts, substance abuse, sexual stunts, compulsive spending, or self-cutting.

Borderlines are people who are NEUROTIC *and* PSYCHOTIC.

It has also been taken to refer to a person who dwells in the margins of sane and insane, destabilizing the false binary system that posits *sane* and *insane* as stark opposites easily separated from each other. The term *borderline* was assigned to those of us who appear normal but have a frightening capacity to regress, obsess, or grow vicious.

A woman with straw in her hair.

A fool with a forehead made of stone.

In her memoir of borderline personality disorder, *Girl, Interrupted,* Susannah Kaysen calls the condition *a way station between neurosis and psychosis: a fractured but not disassembled psyche.* I picture an x-ray of my psyche, veined with hairline cracks. Kaysen says borderline personality is more disturbing than people who talk to themselves on trains or wear hats made of foil to keep government officials from listening to their thoughts. Less obvious versions of madness blur the lines that structure our lives.

Without clear lines how can we know CRAZY from NOT-CRAZY?

How do I know when to get help?

How do you know who was good?

Some people believe borderline personality disorder should be renamed to shift the focus from a spoiled identity to a constellation of symptoms. Borderline personality wears a red miniskirt and smokes magic cigarettes with boys who dream of being wild and wake with cold sweats. She is a WET WILD SEED. Sometimes borderline personality is medical shorthand for patients who make their doctors uncomfortable. Unstable, mercurial, self-injurious, contradictory, seductive, clingy, the term BORDERLINE PERSONALITY has borderline personality. It is in crisis. It is poised to self-destruct.

If diagnosis is narrative, the words for borderline personality may be wrong.

Discussion is underway for revisions to the DSM-V scheduled for release in 2013 and petitions are circulating to replace borderline personality with "emotion regulation disorder," renouncing the label of borderline as insult, injury, and outdated bias on par with hysteria. "Is it by chance," asks one feminist psychoanalytic scholar, "that hysteria (significantly derived . . . from the Greek word for 'uterus') was originally conceived as an exclusively female complaint?"

Madness is a word used to rope a woman's
arms and legs to the bed.

Madness is a metal collar anchoring her to
a cold wall.

The madwoman shrieks and the sound is translated
by some historians as "a response to powerlessness"
in a strange language of protest against a world that
frustrates women by design.

The Mad Pride movement for the acceptance of neurodiversity featured in *Newsweek* in May 2009 continues a radical tradition in psychoanalysis with roots in the work of R. D. Laing, who questioned the social construction of mental illness: "Setting the sick apart sustains the fantasy that we are whole." The idea that anyone is mentally well all of the time is a delusion that gets in the way of asking for help when we find ourselves falling away from our stable minds. Marsha Linehan describes this as the borderline patient's first dilemma:

Am I VULNERABLE AND SAD or UNDISCIPLINED AND BAD?

Linehan holds the contradiction in her hand like it's the unsolved heart of the borderline and asks the patient to look beyond it to more important questions.

DO YOU DESERVE TO FEEL BETTER?
Do you want to pursue your own human potential for fulfillment?

Speaking to the serious social problems of practitioners refusing to treat borderline clients and the media representing women with borderline personality as beautiful sociopaths, in *Through the Looking Glass: Women and Borderline Personality Disorder* Dana Becker urges the public to stop imagining "the borderline client as a 'special case,' unique and strange, as something or someone that needs to be put at a remove." Borderline personality can be construed as a lens that amplifies the self-defeating qualities of normal femininity. Becker encourages nonborder-line women to look through this lens in order "to understand [their] own emotional struggles and the context from which they emerge."

Feminist voices are far from alone in the effort to demystify this disorder. In his roles as director of the International Mood Center at the University of California at San Diego and editor-in-chief of the *Journal of Affective Disorders,* Hagop S. Akiskal points out the unseemly sutures on the Frankenstein face of BORDERLINE PERSONALITY. As an eclectic mix of *traits, symptoms, and behaviors,* the criteria for borderline personality produce *an unwieldy heterogeneity* within the category and overlap with criteria for the affective and addictive disorders. The shared symptoms are rooted in the domain of impulse control: "BOREDOM, EMPTINESS, 'OBJECT HUNGER,' 'ABANDONMENT DEPRESSION,' MERCURIAL MOODS, REACTIVE DYSPHORIA, ANGRY OUTBURSTS, AND IMPULSIVE SUICIDALITY." Joining the efforts of Michael Stone at the Personality Disorders Insti-tute of Columbia University to relocate borderline personality from the subschizophrenic to the subaffective scale of disorder, Akiskal playfully sounds the call for a grassroots feminist psychoanalytic revolution: *All young women unite, you have nothing to lose but your borderline diagnosis.*

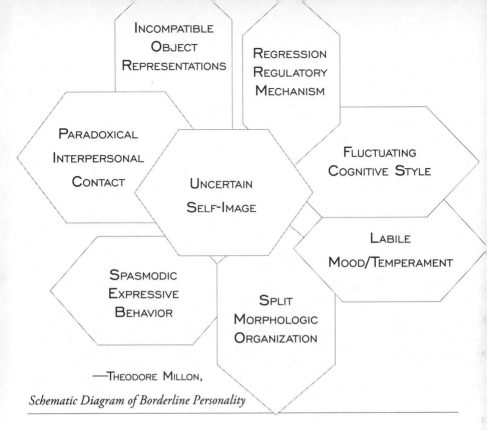

Schematic Diagram of Borderline Personality

This is a risky move.

Proposing that the borderline personality label is INACCURATE or ARTIFICIAL, or that borderlines are NOT CLEARLY DIFFERENT FROM HEALTHY PEOPLE may further undermine the very real needs for therapeutic support and corresponding eligibility for medical insurance claims. These pragmatic concerns cannot be overstated, yet as psychiatric knowledge steadily evolves, identity categories give way to more subtle models that conceptualize mental illness *as dimensions—continua or spectra without clear separation from normalcy, and with less separation from each other than we like to think.*

The whole idea of Axis I and Axis II may prove false and be replaced with the Five-Factor Model of Personality developed by Thomas Widiger, a professor of clinical psychology at the University of Kentucky. Recent discussions of this model were co-authored by Widiger and his colleagues John Livesley, a professor emeritus at the University of British Columbia, and Lee Ana Clark at the University of Iowa, a member of the American Psychological Association committee on personality disorders, which is currently reviewing and revising the content of the DSM-V.

> The benefits of the change from CATEGORY
> to CONTINUUM are vast.

Once questions of CRAZY OR NOT-CRAZY and BORDERLINE OR NOT-BORDERLINE are removed from the table (along with other neurotic distractions like Emily or not-Emily and Mother or not-Mother), a more interesting set of concerns is revealed.

> The process of working through grief and
> loss can begin.

> The facts of attachment disorder, abandonment
> depression, and blocked or incomplete mourning
> surface to explain what was formerly inexplicable.

The repetition compulsion and adrenaline addiction that led me to structure my love life around inevitable loss.

The unspoken bereavement of becoming unsistered that left me clawing the carpet in agony because my stolen girlfriend would not come when called.

If unhealthy attachment styles, personality disorders, and affective dysfunction were recognized as PRODUCTS OF A WIDESPREAD SOCIAL DEFICIT IN EMOTIONAL LITERACY, the headline news that shocks and baffles the general public would no longer be met with surprise. Why do governors cheat on their wives? Why do presidents play doctor with interns? Why does a woman trained to fly to the moon and back let herself be bothered by a boyfriend who chooses someone else over her? Why would she snap and make threats? How does she end up shaking like a leaf?

A personality disorder is not the foreign presence of demonic possession or a cancerous cluster of cells spreading among the internal organs. It is a pattern of cognition and reaction that impairs the capacity to be productive, happy, and generally at ease. It is a fractured sense of self giving way to the weight of stressful interpersonal dynamics.

ATTACHMENT DISORDERS ARE AS COMMON AS DIRT.
They should not be relegated to the speechless realm of the ineffable.

A better understanding can and must be built from materials retrieved from the black holes between words and feelings, past and present, lover and beloved, mental patient and the people who feel perfectly fine. Not everyone that agrees borderline personality is a category beyond repair or a diagnosis preparing to retire.

INCREASING EVIDENCE POINTS TO BORDERLINE PERSONALITY DISORDER AS A VALID DIAGNOSIS WITH RELATIVELY SPECIFIC GENETIC ANTECEDENTS, BIOLOGIC SUSCEPTIBILITIES, PSYCHOSOCIAL ANTECEDENTS, TREATMENT RESPONSE, AND CHARACTERISTIC OUTCOMES. THE SIGNATURE OF BORDERLINE PERSONALITY DISORER IS THE EXQUISITE SENSITIVITY TO THE VICISSITUDES OF INTERPERSONAL RELATIONSHIPS, INCLUDING PROFOUND FEELINGS OF ABANDONMENT UPON DISRUPTION OF THESE RELATIONSHIPS. . . . THE AFFECTIVE SHIFTS IN BORDERLINE PERSONALITY DISORDER, UNLIKE BIPOLAR II, OSCILLATE BETWEEN ANGER AND DYSPHORIA RATHER THAN FROM DEPRESSION TO ELATION AND TEND TO BE REACTIVE TO INTERPERSONAL CONTEXT RATHER THAN ENDOGENOUSLY DRIVEN.

—MARIANNE GOODMAN, ET AL.,

"Quieting the Affective Storm of Borderline Personality Disorder"

Specialists who still believe in the term measure and map neuropsychological phenomena, seeing verbal explosions as microseizures of the frontal lobe supports arguments for BORDERLINE PERSONALITY as a form of EPILEPSY. The acoustic startle eyeblink response has been tested to quantify *the neural circuitry of emotion-processing deficits* in borderlines, adding a solid layer of hard science to the leading argument for renaming borderline personality as a DISORDER OF EMOTION REGULATION—and a corresponding move of the condition from Axis II to Axis I, where bipolar disorder, borderline personality's estranged affective twin, resides.

Other theorists manage the heterogeneity of borderline personality by generating subtypes like siblings to capture the unique faces without denying their family resemblance.

I am one of three sisters who share the diagnosis in our emotional DNA. Our borderline personalities are easily matched with the detailed four-part typology developed by Thedore Millon in his work as director of the Institute for Advanced Studies in Personology and Psychopathology.

DISCOURAGED BORDERLINE (LISA)

By exclusively relying on a single someone, discouraged borderlines "put all their eggs in one basket." Always fearing that their lifeline is threatened, their world is chronically destabilized. Consequently, they are ever preoccupied with their lack of security, mainly their own helplessness, self-doubt, and lack of self-sufficiency. To reinforce their relationships, they cling tenaciously to whoever is available, merging their own identity into that of their partner. Given such profound needs, they are easily panicked by a sense of isolation or aloneness and easily feel depressed and powerless. Simple responsibilities seem monumental, everything is a burden, and life is empty and heavy. Should their sense of futility intensify, they may regress to a state of marked depression or infantile dependency, requiring others to attend to them as if they were infants. They respect authority, tend to be grim and humorless, and expect rewards contingent on compliance and submission. Borderline characteristics begin to develop when the individual senses that this interpersonal pact has been violated too often—that others have selfishly failed to supply promised rewards of affection. Resentful and angry, they no longer believe that conformity will forestall desertion. Instead, they feel coerced into submission and betrayed—emotions that periodically break through normal controls. Because anger is not only inconsistent with their self-image but also alienates or provokes those on whom they depend, intense negative feelings are experienced as dangerous. In response, they may swing to the opposite pole, becoming excessively preoccupied with self-reproach. Self-mutilation and suicidal attempts, symbolic acts of self-desertion, may be used to control their resentment or as punishment for anger.

SELF-DESTRUCTIVE BORDERLINE (JESSICA)

Self-destruction serves the needs of a comorbid masochistic pattern. The self-destructive type is unable to find a comfortable niche with others. Self-destructive borderlines do not become increasingly testy and bitter over time. Instead, their masochistic traits cause them to turn inward, where destructive feelings can be expressed upon the self. These individuals present a veneer of sociability and conformity. Underneath, however, are both a desire for independence and a genuine fear of autonomy. As a result, their social propriety cloaks a deeply conflictful submission to the expectations of others. To control these oppositional tendencies, they struggle to present a facade of self-restraint and self-sacrifice. Ever deferential and ingratiating, most bend over backwards to impress their superiors with their conformity, all the while denying their dependence and becoming even more conflicted. At times, these antagonisms give rise to public displays and bitter complaints about being treated unfairly, to expectations of being disillusioned and disapproved of by others, and to feelings of no longer being appreciated for their diligence, submissiveness, and self-sacrifice. With the persistence of ambivalent feelings, self-destructive borderlines often begin to voice growing distress about a wide range of physical symptoms. As more subtle means of discharging negative feelings prove self-defeating, tension and depression mount beyond tolerable limits. They may accuse others of displeasing them, seeking to destroy their worth, and plotting to abandon them. Inordinate demands for attention and reassurance may be made. They may threaten to commit suicide and thereby save others the energy of destroying them slowly. Self-destructive borderlines (like discouraged borderlines) perpetuate their pathology by deliberately putting themselves in positions of excessive vulnerability, making themselves so dependent and clingy that others can only become exasperated.

IMPULSIVE BORDERLINE (Melissa)

The impulsive borderline is mixed with the histrionic or antisocial pattern. Unless constantly receiving attention, such individuals become increasingly seductive, impulsive, capricious, and irresponsible. Though most borderlines are infamous for dysregulation of negative emotions, subjects with histrionic traits become even more behaviorally hyperactive and cognitively scattered, exhibiting a dysregulation of positive affects that includes frenetic gaiety, frantic gregariousness, and irrational and superficial excitement. At times, they lose all sense of propriety and judgment. Individuals with a stronger antisocial history become even more impulsive and thoughtless, as they struggle to free themselves from social constraints. The impulsive borderline is especially likely to have experienced the chaotic family or soap opera environment, which encourages drama, a desire for stimulus variety, and an intolerance to boredom. Many will have felt a sense of security and attachment only when their parents acknowledged some exhibitionistic performance or when their misbehavior was intense enough to stand out against the background noise of chaos and discord. They fail to develop a solid self-identity that might anchor them during periods of stress. As a consequence, they are always on unsure footing, constantly on edge, never quite sure who will provide the attention and stimulation they desperately require.

Our three primary types are marbled with fat veins of PETULANCE. We are STUBBORN. DEMANDING. BITTER. AGITATED. VICIOUS. INDIGNANT. HOSTILE. Angry at a childhood in which we were mishandled, cheated, and caught in a power struggle between parents. The petulant borderline is our gangster alter ego.

A switchblade in the pocket. Flash of psychosis in the eye.

Unable to find comfort with others, they may become increasingly bitter and discontent. They express feelings of worthlessness and futility, become highly agitated or deeply depressed, express self-condemnation, and develop delusions of guilt. Their habitual negativism becomes completely irrational, driving them into rages in which they distort reality, make excessive demands of others, and viciously attack those they see as having trapped them and forced them into intolerable conflicts. Their moods become a way of threatening others that further trouble is coming unless something is done.

—Theodore Millon,
Personality Disorders in Modern Life

Spasmodic. Paradoxical. Mercurial. Ego-Dystonic.

We become hysterical. We dissociate. We perseverate.

We get too close too fast and wait for the one we love to cheat and devastate. Or we grow to hate our husbands and wives for hijacking our lives. Jump from the moving car. Believe we are saving ourselves.

I leave Emily. I leave town. I calm down. I bury my unresolved neurotic conflicts for another day.

I BROKE UP WITH EMILY and my tact left much to be desired.

I wish I could say I WOKE UP / GOT HELP / SAW GOD / MADE AMENDS / DID THE RIGHT THING / BECAME A BETTER PERSON / START-ED A NONPROFIT DEDICATED TO SERVING OTHERS.

BORDERLINES WITHOUT BORDERS.

If I were a nonprofit organization the more fitting name would be BORDERLINES WITHOUT MANNERS. Emily left Vanessa for me but I no longer wanted her. It was too late. I was too hurt. I dread this part of the story. I know people will say I only want what I can't have. They will only be partly right. There is more to my reason for dropping the obsession with Emily.

There is more to the moment of No that finally arrived inside me.

By the time Emily offered to become not just lovers but partners and family with me, I had realized we were emotionally incompatible. Her need for emotional privacy conflicted with my need for emotional transparency. If I stayed with her I would always burn with anxiety in my stomach, haunted by the fear that she was wandering with others, pressing her lips to someone else's, keeping the details of her daily business from me just to know she could. I had been waiting for the affair to end, thinking I would be free of anxiety, but something dawned on me that spring. Being with Emily *is* being anxious.

Every day would be her birthday trip to Asheville.
The long December weekend when she would not
tell anyone where she planned to stay—not her
partner, not her lover, not her therapist.

She needs a secret compartment in her relationship. That's the only way she feels solid and whole behind the corporate edifice of lesbian union. I could not foresee living happily with an opaque window of a wife, and I no longer wanted to proceed with the sad masquerade of stolen goods as stable domesticity. The time had come to put right what I got wrong. When the decision to disentangle myself from Emily takes up permanent residence in my body—after two years of coming and going like a tramp—it displaces a lump of anxiety lodged in my lungs since I was a young girl. If being with Emily *is* being anxious, the equation must also indicate that being *myself* is being anxious. I draw a breath so deep it surprises me. The stone of folly has been retrieved from my roughly cracked chest.

This crack in your façade can be the first glimpse
you have had to your real self. Ironically, your newly
experienced vulnerability—the feeling that you are
now exposed for all the world to see, that all your
weaknesses are now visible—is the very thing that
can save you.

Beneath the facades of distraction, debauchery, denial, and diagnosis, a deeper level of unsolved heartsore questions about mental health flows. Here is where the hard work truly begins. I set out to make friends with my borderline personality. I set out to teach my borderline personality to play well with others.

HALFWAY HOUSE FOR THE BRIGHT BUT BROKENHEARTED

YOUR SHIP MAY BE COMING IN

YOU'RE WEAK BUT NOT GIVING IN

TO THE CRIES AND THE WAILS OF THE VALLEY BELOW

—RILO KILEY, "Better Son/Daughter"

I am sitting in the tub with my wife, hoping to steam anxiety from the muscles between my shoulders where I hold grief and neurosis in a series of knots. S/he faces me from the faucet end of the tub, nodding and making soothing noises and listening to me talk about my sister. Less than six months have passed since Stace and I stood in a gazebo in Easthampton, Massachusetts, to exchange vows on a sunny afternoon in May while Jessica snapped photos. A stranger said, "Nice day for a wedding," as she walked by the small park next to city hall.

My sister's wife, Misty, did not attend the wedding.

She called us copycats behind our backs and hid upstairs in her study while we toasted our wedding night with glasses of scotch in the living room below. I think of Misty as Stepmonster #3—yet another woman who married into my family and then wedged herself between my sister and me—and last Christmas when I spent the holiday with the two of them I told Jessica how sad I felt about her marriage and the way it replayed the dynamics of our childhood separation. The wedding visit in May triggered painful memories again and I sobbed into my pillow while my new spouse rubbed my back and swore never to let me spend another night under a roof where I did not feel welcome.

———

Tonight I am reeling after a week of keeping constant tabs on Jessica.

When my sisters hurt, I do too. When my sisters can't eat, neither can I. My response to crisis in their lives is always excessive. I panic. I obsess. I can't stop worrying. Jessica has lived through plenty of difficult experiences but this week threatens to be the worst.

MISTY CHEATED ON HER.

Then asked for divorce via text message.

Jessica is handling her pain gracefully. Within days she finds a nice vintage apartment, consults an attorney, meets old friends for coffee, changes her name to Jay, and speaks calmly to me on the phone about her glad feelings of being free from a spouse who isolated and berated her during most of their five-year relationship. She is looking forward to pursuing new friendships and healthier romantic partnerships. I tell her I am in awe of her clarity and resilience, but the pressure of worrying about her this week hits me in the hot water of the tub and I hold my face in my hands until Stace says we should dry off and watch a movie and fall asleep.

I check my phone as I sit down on the edge of the bed.
I have a text from Jay. A suicide text.

> Please kill me? I need to leave my life.
>
> I am doing everything I can to keep myself alive.

> Do you think I should check into a
>
> place that could help me? I need to
>
> call my doctor. Please help me.

I call her and find myself in a four-way phone conversation with Jay, our father who rarely talks to Jay, and Misty's mother who talks to ghosts. It turns out Jay's grace was a cover. The truth is she's falling apart. She hasn't eaten in five days. She's barely sleeping. She slurs her words. She's drinking from the bottle.

"Too kill her."

No.

"Tequila."

She wants to die. She wonders if she should take all the pills in the house. I stay on the phone until the ambulance arrives and takes her to the hospital to treat her for malnourishment and stabilize her mental state. The next morning she makes an emergency appointment with her nurse practitioner for medication to get through this crisis. When she returns home, someone knocks on the door. The police. Misty took out a restraining order and Jay has fifteen minutes to leave by police escort. She takes her dog and some clothes and calls me from the side of the road. Stace gets on a plane to rescue her and drives her thirteen hours back to our home in South Carolina.

I put a card on her bed with a monkey dressed like a nurse.

Welcome to the Haney-Johnson Halfway House for the Bright but Brokenhearted.

I put flowers on the desk in our purple guest room. I bring her small plates of pineapple and pick out movies for her to watch. At night I tuck her in as if she's a child and put my hand on her face like I'm checking for fever, then sit on the edge of her bed and talk for a while before kissing her goodnight.

One thing we talk about is our other sister, Melissa. She is hospitalized in Atlanta because she has cancer. She is bleeding so much from the rectum she has to wear diapers. She can't keep anything on her stomach because the chemo nauseates her. She has known about the cancer for more than a year but never told us. She didn't want treatment. She didn't want reality. She ran away from her third husband to live with a man who would beat her every day and break her phone on the hood of his truck so she couldn't call anyone for help. She got away from him after a few months and went back home where she finally got too sick to hide it. Melissa called me from the hospital room a few days before the suicide text from Jay. I reserved a hotel room in Atlanta and planned to visit her the following day.

That night Melissa goes missing. No one knows where she is.
Stace and I cancel our hotel reservations and wait for more news.

When Melissa resurfaces we struggle to make the pieces of her story fit together. She is so sick she can't eat and wears diapers, but she has been discharged from the hospital and is staying with a friend and says she hopes we still come to Atlanta so she can hang out with us in the hotel and get away from it all. I feel a familiar heaviness in my abdomen. Mistrust. I grow wary and distant. I mask my true feelings when she calls. I still want to be a safe place for her. When she says she wants to come to my house I feel a cord stretch between my body and hers, and I want her here where I can take care of her, even though I'm coming down with the flu and have a writing project that's way overdue.

There's no reason to worry.

She won't come.

Melissa tells me she started writing again recently. She tells me she
has tumors in her colon and she's probably going to die. She tells me her
sons will go crazy when we put her in the ground. She tells me to watch
the oldest one closely. She tells me painful things that tear me up inside.
Loss burrows inside her psyche like a splinter of glass and comes out her
face in lies.

She is a WALKING WISH PSYCHOSIS.

I don't know if she has cancer. I don't know if she still writes poems
or if she just makes things up. She is a ghost face. She is a pocket of blood
ready to burst.

I can't fix her.

I can't fix the world that hurt her.

Hurting for her is a way to avoid the less attractive
truth of hurting for myself.

IN THE WORDS of Judith Herman, my "intimate relationships" have been "driven by the hunger for protection and care" and have been "haunted by the fear of abandonment or exploitation." After years of "repeatedly enacting dramas of rescue, injustice, and betrayal"—

> you look like a perfect fit, for a girl in need
>
> of a tourniquet, but can you save me?

—I see where my capacity for despair, obsession, and self-destruction comes from. The pain caused by years of secretly suspecting something was wrong with me surprises me by subsiding when I realize something *is* in fact wrong.

I'M NOT CRAZY FOR FEELING CRAZY.

Bedtime stories and fairy tales are filled with thickets of thorns and girls with blood flowing from their fingertips like ink. I have searched one hundred years for a person to inscribe my body with a curlicue ending of *happily ever after*.

I have paid my dues. I have waited for my reward.

This year I won the prize and became the bride but let me tell you something, Reader. A wedding is no cure for attachment disorder. I still break things sometimes. I still yell. I still hold my knees to my chest and rock myself into a trance. The card with the monkey nurse belongs as much on my bed as on my sister's. If this is a halfway house for the easily triggered and emotionally impaired, I am its longest resident. The arts and crafts sessions of taking care of Jay are therapy for my own cross-addicted mind. The everyday conflicts of my marriage with Stacey is a kind of couples therapy, pushing me to grow and gain confidence in navigating emotional storms with a steady hand. We have been hosting Jay for several weeks now and our time together will soon end. She will drive back to Massachusetts and follow the scattered threads of her new life as she grieves the loss of her old one, and I will miss her. The work all three of us have done this month in negotiating boundaries and forming bonds of mutual support must be something like what happens in rehab.

Stace puts a pan of water on the stove to boil for spaghetti noodles.

Jay lights a cigarette on the patio off the kitchen and says, "The sky looks kind of pink like when it snows in Massachusetts."

I take a deep breath at my desk and exhale a lungful of hope for Melissa's health. Then I write the last sentences of my book and harness our pups for a brisk walk.

Each of us makes tentative steps towards wellness.

I watch the light in the sky deepen from pink to plum and wait for a better season.

ACKNOWLEDGMENTS

I OWE SO MUCH to so many people for supporting me in my personal and professional life during the long struggle to bring this book to completion. The biggest acknowledgement goes to my spouse, Stace, who took on all the most unpleasant tasks of keeping me in writerly condition: managing technological snafus, panic attacks, late night snacks, and romantic rendezvous. My sister Jay is a soldier and a role model and I can't wait to see the book she is destined to write. My sister Melissa has poetry in her and I still hope to see her put it all into words. My father, mother, and grandma have also cheered me on and dared me to tell the whole truth. My far-flung community of women writers—Deborah Siegel, Jennifer Baumgardner, Daphne Gottlieb, Drue Barker, Alison

Piepmeier, Lara Stemple, Laura Mazer, Kathy Belden, Rosemary Daniell, and Amy Blackmarr—have networked me and stretched me and consoled me and encouraged me to be bolder. My colleagues at USC Upstate—Theresa Ricke-Kiely, Rachel Snow, Kevin Mulhearn, Clif Flynn, York Bradshaw, and Warren Carson—have taught me almost as much as my therapists. My therapists—Helen and Pam—never flinched. Many of my students performed tirelessly in the reading of drafts, offering insights and wisdom beyond their years and morphing over time into dear friends—Andrea Miller, Jason Funderburk, Adrienne Jones, Megan Wood, and Leigh Hendrix. The preparation of the manuscript was a complex process, and I am grateful for the editorial talent, creative vision, patience, and kindness of the Seal Press team: Krista Lyons, Krissa Lagos, Andie East, and Domini Dragoone. For last minute help on matters large and small, I could not wish for better than my current research assistant, Beth TeVault, generously funded by the Honors Program at USC Upstate, under the discretion of another very thoughtful and supportive colleague, Tom McConnell. And last but not least, my loyal companions Millie and Lola made each writing day a little warmer.

ENDNOTES

AUTHOR'S NOTE: Source materials have been edited in some cases for clarity, conciseness, and gendered pronoun usage. In other cases, sources have been treated as found poems, editing syntax, punctuation, and progression of ideas with poetic license (marked below as "based on" source material). The integrity of content has been preserved for all sources.

FRONT MATTER
You look like a perfect fit . . .
Aimee Mann, "Save Me" (*Magnolia Soundtrack*, Warner Brothers, 1999).

A borderline suffers a kind of emotional hemophilia . . .
Jerold Kriesman and Hal Straus, *I Hate You, Don't Leave Me: Understanding the Borderline Personality* (New York: Avon, 1991), 8.

CHAPTER I
UNSOLVED HEART
p. 11   *Whatever's burning in me is mine . . .*
Toni Morrison, *Sula* (New York: Penguin, 1973), 93.

Things went from bad to worse . . .
William Plummer, "In the Heat of the Night." *People Magazine* 27 June 1997: 36-37.

Left Eye didn't mean to burn the house down . . .
The Last Days of Left Eye, Dir. Lauren Lazin (Starz Studio, 2008).

p. 14   *Be patient toward all that is unsolved . . .*
Rainer Maria Rilke, "Letter No. 4." Trans. M. D. Herter. *Letters to a Young Poet* (New York: Norton, 1934), 11.

p. 16   *poetcrippledead*
Based on Anne Sexton, "The Farmer's Wife." *To Bedlam and Part Way Back* (New York: Houghton Mifflin, 1960), 27. Lines 28-32.

p. 18   *They tell it like I was just crazy drunk out my mind . . .*
The Last Days of Left Eye, Dir. Lauren Lazin (Starz Studio, 2008).

p. 20   *How you know?" Sula asked . . .*
Toni Morrison, *Sula* (New York: Penguin, 1973), 146.

Chapter 2
ATTACHMENT THIEF
p. 31   *The "Strange Situation" was the label assigned . . .*
Mary D. Salters Ainsworth, et al., *Patterns of Attachment: A Psychological Study of the Strange Situation* (Hillsdale, NJ: Lawrence Erlbaum, 1978), viii.

p. 32   *attachment gone awry . . .*
Robert Jensen, *Becoming Attached: First Relationships and How They Shape Our Capacity to Love* (Oxford: Oxford UP, 1998), 380.

p. 33   *Hazan–Shaver Adult Attachment Interview*
Cindy Hazan and Philip R. Shaver, "Romantic Love Conceptualized as an Attachment Process." *Journal of Personality and Social Psychology* 52.3 (1987): 511-24.

p. 36   *Apprehensive movements, fearful expressions . . .*
Mary Main and Erik Hesse, "Parents's Unresolved Traumatic Experiences Are Related to Infant Disorganized Attachment Status: Is Frightened and/or Frightening Parental Behavior the Linking Mechanism?" *Attachment in the Preschool Years: Theory, Research and Intervention.* Eds. Mark T. Greenberg, Dante Cicchetti, and E. Mark Cummings (Chicago: U of Chicago P, 1990), 173.

p. 38   *two dimensional model of interpersonal style*
Kim Bartholomew and Leonard Horowitz, "Attachment Styles among Young Adults: A Test of a Four-Category Model." *Journal of Personality and Social Psychology* 61.2 (1991): 227.

p. 52   *Just as the cuckold was known by his horns . . .*
Roy Porter, *Madness: A Brief History* (Oxford: Oxford UP, 2002), 64.

Imago. Ghost partner. Parent image . . .
Based on Harville Hendrix, *Keeping the Love You Find: A Personal Guide* (New York: Atria, 1992), 21.

p. 54   *If you think I'm sexy . . .*
Rod Stewart, "Da Ya Think I'm Sexy?" *Blondes Have More Fun* (Warner Brothers, 1978).

p. 58   *Boom I got your boyfriend . . .*
M. C. Luscious. "Boom! I Got Your Boyfriend." *Boom!* (Heatwave Records, 1991).

CHAPTER 3
RUBYFRUIT MASOCHIST
p. 63   *The match ignites. The unconscious falls in love . . .*
Based on Harville Hendrix, *Keeping the Love You Find: A Personal Guide* (New York: Atria, 1992), 21.

p. 70   *three-dimensional representations of the psychological space . . .*
Laura Camille Tuley, "Our Lovely Prisons: The Performance of Female Perversions in Daphne Loney's Sculpture." *New Orleans Review* 27.2 (2001): 120-21.

not about the oppression but about the participation of women . . .
Laura Camille Tuley, "Our Lovely Prisons: The Performance of Female Perversions in Daphne Loney's Sculpture." *New Orleans Review* 27.2 (2001): 121, 124.

p. 74   *Pseudo-love. If a person has not reached the level . . .*
Based on Erich Fromm, *The Art of Loving* (New York: Harper and Row, 1956), 99-100.

p. 76   *The collars are made of metal . . .*
Based on Laura Camille Tuley, "Our Lovely Prisons: The Performance of Female Perversions in Daphne Loney's Sculpture." *New Orleans Review* 27.2 (2001): 124.

CHAPTER 4
HYSTERICAL PAROXYSM
p. 78   *Robert Frost says good fences make good neighbors . . .*
Robert Frost, "Mending Wall." *North of Boston* (New York: Holt, 1914), 11-13.

. . . but everyone knows he secretly fantasizes about swinging from birches.
Robert Frost, "Birches." *Mountain Interval* (New York: Holt, 1916), 37-40.

p. 79   *Like a sponge, the mate with boundaries set too close . . .*
Anne Katherine, *Boundaries: Where You End and I Begin* (New York: Fireside, 1991), 123.

p. 80   *Maureen stays calm and rinses the vegetables . . .*
Anne Katherine, *Where To Draw the Line: How To Set Healthy Boundaries Every Day* (New York: Fireside, 2000), 93.

p. 83   *Anxiety; excessive need for affection . . .*
Karen Horney, *The Neurotic Personality of Our Time* (New York: Norton, 1937), 138.

p. 84   *With the infallibility of a sleepwalker . . .*
Alice Miller, *The Drama of the Gifted Child: The Search for the True Self* (New York: Basic, 1981), 99.

p. 86   *I think I love you . . .*
The Partridge Family, "I Think I Love You." *I Think I Love You* (Bell Records, 1970).

p. 88   *If you are in a relationship where you feel great swings in feelings . . .*
Howard Halpern, *How to Break Your Addiction to a Person: When and Why Love Doesn't Work and What to Do about It* (New York: McCraw, 1982), 71.

p. 91   *Take this job and shove it . . .*
Johnny Paycheck, "Take this Job and Shove It." *Take this Job and Shove It* (Epic Records, 1977).

p. 92   *As a rule, the relationship from which she expects heaven on earth . . .*
Karen Horney, *Our Inner Conflicts: A Constructive Theory of Neurosis* (New York: Norton, 1945), 61-62.

p. 93   *All my integrity seemed to lie in saying No . . .*
Susannah Kaysen, *Girl, Interrupted* (New York: Random House, 1993), 42.

p. 94   *"I would prefer not to," he says . . .*
Herman Melville, "Bartleby, the Scrivener: A Story of Wall-Street" (*Putnam's Monthly*, November 1853; Rpt. *Billy Budd, Sailor and Selected Tales*, Oxford: Oxford UP, 1998), 12.

p. 94   *pathogenic environment . . .*
Jules Henry, *Pathways to Madness* (New York: Random House, 1965), 372-73.

p. 96   *They pile up over time . . .*
Based on Herman Melville, "Bartleby, the Scrivener: A Story of Wall-Street" (*Putnam's Monthly*, November 1853; Rpt. *Billy Budd, Sailor and Selected Tales*, Oxford: Oxford UP, 1998), 41.

p. 97   *He calls Bartleby an inscrutable text . . .*
Herman Melville, "Bartleby, the Scrivener: A Story of Wall-Street" (*Putnam's Monthly*, November 1853; Rpt. *Billy Budd, Sailor and Selected Tales*, Oxford: Oxford UP, 1998), 28.

CHAPTER 5
THE GIFT OF SELF-DESTRUCTION
p. 101   *The complex of melancholia behaves like an open wound . . .*
Sigmund Freud, "Mourning and Melancholia," *Collected Papers, Vol. IV: Papers on Metapsychology and Applied Psycho-analysis*, Ed. E. Jones (London: Hogarth, 1995), 253.

p. 102   *Neuropsychiatry calls this recklessness a fatal flaw . . .*
Stuart Yudovsky, *Fatal Flaws: Navigating Destructive Relationships with People with Disorders of Personality and Character* (Washington, DC: American Psychiatric Publishing, 2005), 5-7.

a stand in, a stop-gap, a mask . . .
Ann Marlowe, *How to Stop Time: Heroin from A to Z* (New York: Basic, 1999), 155.

p. 103   *Barriers also seem to provoke this madness . . .*
Helen Fisher, *Anatomy of Love: A Natural History of Mating, Marriage, and Why We Stray* (New York: Norton, 1992), 48.

p. 105   *If I get stoned and sing all night long . . .*
Hank Williams, Jr., "Family Tradition." *Family Tradition* (Curb Records, 1979).

p. 106   *For now, I hold love on my tongue . . .*
Nancy Mairs, *Remembering the Bone House: An Erotics of Place and Space* (Boston: Beacon, 1989), 248.

p. 108   *Addictive relationships are marked by their endurance . . .*
Peele, Stanton. "Fools for Love: The Romantic Ideal, Psychological Theory, and Addictive Love." *The Psychology of Love*. Ed. R. J. Sternberg (New Haven, CT: Yale   UP, 1989), 169.

p. 111   *One response to feeling abandoned . . .*
Theodore Millon, *Personality Disorders in Modern Life*, 2nd ed. (Hoboken, NJ: John Wiley and Sons, 2004), 500.

complementary transactions . . .
Thomas A. Harris, *I'm OK, You're OK* (New York: Harper, 1969), 80.

p. 112   *The person whose not ok child is always activated . . .*
Thomas A. Harris, *I'm OK, You're OK* (New York: Harper, 1969), 88.

p. 114   *Where the patient errs . . .*
Horney, Karen. *Our Inner Conflicts: A Constructive Theory of Neurosis* (New York: Norton, 1945), 51.

p. 117   *I'm a beast. I go mad . . .*
Based on Radclyffe Hall, *The Well of Loneliness* (London: Cape, 1928), 147.

p. 117   *The child wants immediate results . . .*
Based on Thomas A. Harris, *I'm OK, You're OK* (New York: Harper, 1969), 53.

p. 118   *You would be well advised not to believe him* . . .
Howard Halpern, *How to Break your Addiction to a Person: When and Why Love Doesn't Work and What to Do about It* (New York: McCraw, 1982), 180.

p. 119   *Stephen was blinded by stardust and love stories* . . .
Based on Radclyffe Hall, *The Well of Loneliness* (London: Cape, 1928), 146.

Because we love each other so deeply. Because we're perfect . . .
Based on Radclyffe Hall, *The Well of Loneliness* (London: Cape, 1928), 145.

p. 120   *Stephen went and knelt beside her* . . .
Based on Radclyffe Hall, *The Well of Loneliness* (London: Cape, 1928), 156-57.

p. 124   *All I know in love is how to shock people* . . .
Lisa Crystal Carver, *Drugs Are Nice: A Post Punk Memoir* (Brooklyn: Soft Skull, 1995), 246.

p. 130   *I have lived on the lip of insanity* . . .
Rumi, Jalal al-Din. *Unseen Rain: Quatrains of Rumi.* Trans. John Moyne and Coleman Barks (Boston: Shambala, 2001), 75.

There is a difference between love and human sacrifice . . .
Nancy Mairs, *Plaintext: Deciphering a Woman's Life* (Boston: Beacon, 1992), 122.

"Self-attack thus represents a 'gift of love' intended to satisfy vicious introjects . . ."
Theodore Millon, *Personality Disorders in Modern Life*, 2nd ed. (Hoboken, NJ: Wiley, 2004), 501.

fantasies can be examined . . .
Theodore Millon, *Personality Disorders in Modern Life*, 2nd ed. (Hoboken, NJ: Wiley, 2004), 514.

p. 131   *Sometimes you don't choose things. They just happen.* . . .
"Exclusive: Read Emails between Sanford, Woman." *The State* (June 25, 2009): http://www.thestate.com/2009/06/25839350/exclusive-read-e-mails-between. html, (Accessed August 30, 2009).

p. 131   *The writing is on the wall . . .*
Peter Hamby, "Sanford Rejects Call for Resignation from Lieutenant Governor." *CNNPolitics.com* (August 26, 2009): http://www.cnn.com/2009/POLITICS/08/26/mark.sanford/ (Accessed August 30, 2009).

CHAPTER 6
ROCKET GIRL
p. 133   *I think Amelia had it okay . . .*
Deb Talan, "Thinking Amelia." *Something Burning* (CD Baby, 2000).

p. 134   BIOGRAPHICAL DETAILS OF PRINCESS DIANA
Sally Bedell Smith, *Diana in Search of Herself: Portrait of a Troubled Princess* (New York: Penguin, 1999).

p. 139   CRITERIA FOR BORDERLINE PERSONALITY DISORDER
American Psychiatric Association, *Diagnostic and Statistical Manual of Mental Disorders*, 4th edition, Text Revision (Washington, DC, American Psychiatric Association, 2000).

p. 140   BIOGRAPHICAL DETAILS OF CAMILLE CLAUDEL
Odile Ayral-Clause, *Camille Claudel: A Life* (New York: Harry N. Abrams, Inc., 2002).

p. 144   *The borderline does not accept her own intelligence . . .*
Jerold Kreisman and Hal Straus, *I Hate You, Don't Leave Me: Understanding the Borderline Personality* (New York: Avon, 1991), 35.

p. 149   *"spoken and unspoken, reasonable and unreasonable" . . .*
Alice Miller, *The Drama of the Gifted Child: The Search for the True Self* (New York: Basic, 1981), 99.

p. 150   *Both respond to real or perceived deprivation with oral sadism . . .*
Lawrence Kayton, "The Relationship of the Vampire Legend to Schizophrenia." *Journal of Youth and Adolescence* 1.4 (1972): 303-14.

p. 152   *For it is only the suppression of justified rage in childhood . . .*
Alice Miller, *The Drama of the Gifted Child: The Search for the True Self* (New York: Basic, 1981), 4.

p. 154   *Of course she drove fourteen hours straight through the night . . .*
Alex Tresniowski, et al., "Out of This World." *People Magazine* (February 19, 2007),   58-63.

p. 156   3 LEVELS OF EMOTIONAL FUNCTIONING
John Gunderson, *Borderline Personality Disorder: A Clinical Guide* (Arlington, VA: American Psychiatric Publishing, 2008), 32-37.

CHAPTER 7
TANTRUM ARTIST
p. 160   *bark against the Dog Star . . .*
Anonymous, "Loving Mad Tom" (1656). Rpt. *A Mind Apart: Poems of Melancholy, Madness, and Addiction.* Ed. Mark S. Bauer (Oxford: Oxford UP, 2009), 91-92.

p. 161   *The only thing I want to say . . .*
Sarah Kane, *Sarah Kane: Complete Plays* (London: Metheun Drama, 2001), p. 172.

I tell him he is a flower that blossomed in a mud puddle . . .
Stephen Crane, *Maggie: A Girl of the Streets* (New York: Appleton, 1896), 38.

p. 163   *You're the only one . . .*
Phil Collins, "Against All Odds." *Against All Odds Soundtrack* (Atlantic Records, 1984).

p. 171   *Tantrum behavior can be traced back to childhood relationships . . .*
Theodore Millon, *Personality Disorders in Modern Life*, 2nd ed. (Hoboken, NJ: John Wiley and Sons, 2004).

p. 179   Evelyn Lau, *Oedipal Dreams* (Vancouver: Beach Holme, 1992).

p. 182   *Doesn't take much to rip us into pieces . . .*
Tori Amos, "Crucify." *Little Earthquakes* (Atlantic Records, 1992).

p. 183   *To live a life analogous to a soap opera . . .*
Theodore Millon, *Personality Disorders in Modern Life*, 2nd ed. (Hoboken, NJ: John Wiley and Sons, 2004), 478.

p. 184   *Borderlines create the vicious circles they fear most* . . .
Theodore Millon, *Personality Disorders in Modern Life*, 2nd ed. (Hoboken, NJ: John Wiley and Sons, 2004), 498.

p. 185   *pride in the power of self-destruction* . . .
Otto F. Kernberg, *Borderline Conditions and Pathological Narcissism* (New York: Jason Aronson, 1975), 125.

To ease tension; to express emotional pain . . .
Marilee Strong, *A Bright Red Scream: Self-Mutilation and the Language of Pain* (New York: Penguin, 1999), 162.

In everyday life it is possible to obtain some respite . . .
Armando Favazza, *Bodies under Siege: Self-Mutilation and Body Modification in Culture and Psychiatry* (Baltimore, MD: Johns Hopkins UP, 1987), 272.

p. 188   *Kettlewell describes her recovery in terms of neural pathways* . . .
Caroline Kettlewell, *Skin Game: A Memoir* (New York: St. Martin's, 2000), 97, 178.

A twenty-two-year-old woman named Dominique Fisher in England . . .
Daily Mail Reporter, "Woman Who Carved Her Name into Lover's Arm during Drug-Fuelled Fling Walks Free." *Daily Mail* (March 20, 2009). http://www.dailymail.co.uk/news/article-1163483/Woman-carved-lovers-arm-drug-fueled-fling-walks-free-court.html (Accessed June 25, 2009).

CHAPTER 8
BECOMING BORDERLINE

p. 191   *The shimmering, ever-shifting borderline like all boundaries beckons* . . .
Susannah Kaysen, *Girl, Interrupted* (New York: Random House, 1993), 159.

p. 193   *Once one is properly wearied* . . .
Stephen Crane, "The Open Boat" (1898). *Great Short Works of Stephen Crane* (New York: Harper Perennial, 2004), 300.

p. 195   *just a shape to fill a lack . . . Sin and love and fear are just sounds* . . .
William Faulkner, *As I Lay Dying* (New York: Vintage, 1991), 172-74.

p. 196   "...the insane have standardly been depicted as..."
Roy Porter, *Madness: A Brief History* (Oxford: Oxford UP, 2002), 64.

p. 197   *a way station between neurosis and psychosis*...
Susannah Kaysen, *Girl, Interrupted* (New York: Random House, 1993), 151.

p. 198   *"Is it by chance," asks one feminist psychoanalytic scholar..."*
Shoshana Felman, *What Does a Woman Want? Reading and Sexual Difference* (Baltimore, MD: Johns Hopkins UP, 1993), 20-21.

p. 199   *The Mad Pride movement for the acceptance of neurodiversity*...
Alissa Quart, "Listening to Madness." *Newsweek* (May 2, 2009).

Setting the sick apart sustains the fantasy...
Roy Porter, *Madness: A Brief History* (Oxford: Oxford UP, 2002), 63.

Am I vulnerable and sad or undisciplined and bad?
Marsha M. Linehan, *Cognitive-Behavioral Treatment of Borderline Personality Disorder* (New York: Guilford, 1993), 74.

Speaking to the serious social problems of practitioners refusing to treat borderline...
Dana Becker, *Through the Looking Glass: Women and Borderline Personality Disorder* New Directions in Theory and Psychology Series (Boulder, CO: Westview, 1997), 118.

p. 200   *As an eclectic mix of traits, symptoms, and behaviors*
Hagop Akiskal, "Demystifying Borderline Personality: Critique of the Concept and Unorthodox Reflections on Its Natural Kinship with the Bipolar Spectrum." *Acta Psychiatrica Scandinavia* 110 (2004): 401-07.

p. 201   SCHEMATIC DIAGRAM OF BORDERLINE PERSONALITY
Theodore Millon, "Capricious/Borderline." Institute for Advanced Studies in Personology and Psychopathology. http://www.million.net//taxonomy/borderline/htm (Accessed December 1, 2009).

as dimensions—continua or spectra without clear separation from normalcy...
Mark S. Bauer, *A Mind Apart: Poems of Melancholy, Madness, and Addiction.* Ed. Mark S. Bauer (Oxford: Oxford UP, 2009), 5.

p. 202   *Five-Factor Model of Personality . . .*
Thomas Widiger, John Livesley, and Lee Ana Clark, "An Integrative Dimensional Classification of Personality Disorder." *Psychological Assessment* 21.3 (2009): 243-55.

p. 203   *personality disorder is not the foreign presence of demonic possession . . .*
Michael Annestis, "A Dimensional Model of Personality Disorders: Moving towards DSM-V." *Psychotherapy Brown Bag Blog: Discussing the Science of Clinical Psychology* (September 23, 2009). http://www.psychotherapybrownbag.com/psychotherapy_brown_bag_a/2009/09/a-dimensional-model-of-personlaity-disorders-moving-towards-dsmv.html, (Accessed December 1, 2009).

p. 204   *points to borderline personality disorder as a valid diagnosis . . .*
Marianne Goodman, et al., "Quieting the Affective Storm of Borderline Personality."

p. 205   *borderline personality as a form of epilepsy . . .*
Catherine L. Harris, et al., "Partial Seizure-Like Symptoms in Borderline Personality Disorder." *Epilepsy and Behavior* 3 (2002): 433-38.

acoustic startle eyeblink response has been tested to quantify . . .
E. Hazlett, et al., "Exaggerated Affect-Modulated Startle During Unpleasant Stimuli in Borderline Personality Disorder." *Biological Psychiatry* 62.3 (2007): 250-255.

p. 205   DISCOURAGED BORDERLINE
Theodore Millon, *Personality Disorders in Modern Life*, 2nd ed. (Hoboken, NJ: John Wiley and Sons, 2004), 483-84.

p. 207   SELF-DESTRUCTIVE BORDERLINE
Theodore Millon, *Personality Disorders in Modern Life*, 2nd ed. (Hoboken, NJ: John Wiley and Sons, 2004), 488.

p. 208   IMPULSIVE BORDERLINE
Theodore Millon, *Personality Disorders in Modern Life*, 2nd ed. (Hoboken, NJ: John Wiley and Sons, 2004), 484-85.

p. 210   PETULANT BORDERLINE
Theodore Millon, *Personality Disorders in Modern Life*, 2nd ed. (Hoboken, NJ: John Wiley and Sons, 2004), 486-88.

p. 212   *This crack in your façade can be the first glimpse . . .*
Beverly Engel, *The Jekyll and Hyde Syndrome: What to Do if Someone in Your Life Has a Dual Personality—or if You Do.* (Hoboken, NJ: John Wiley and Sons, 2007), 248-49.

Chapter 9
HALFWAY HOUSE FOR THE BRIGHT BUT BROKENHEARTED

p. 215   *Your ship may be coming in . . .*
Rilo Kiley, "Better Son/Daughter." *The Execution of All Things* (Saddle Creek Records, 2002).

p. 221   *my intimate relations have been driven by the hunger for . . .*
Judith Herman, *Trauma and Recovery* (New York: Basic, 1992), 111.

READING GUIDE

1. In *Girl in Need of a Tourniquet*, Merri Lisa Johnson describes a breakthrough in the writing process that comes when she stops asking herself who was right and who was wrong (in her family of origin and in her devastating romantic affair with Emily). How does her perspective change when she rejects the narrow stories of victim vs. villain or right vs. wrong and approaches her personal narrative from another place? How would you describe this third option or "other place"? Is Johnson successful in departing from the limited options of accusation or atonement? Are there moments in the book that indicate her former tendency towards splitting—seeing a person or thing as all good or all bad—before she experiences the cognitive breakthrough described in the opening chapter?

2. Throughout *Girl in Need of a Tourniquet*, the personal narrative is punctuated by portraits of celebrities, media scandals, and literary characters with whom the author identifies, and whose stories she retells in unusual ways. What is the effect of these sections of the book? How do they advance the author's story? How do they affect the reading experience? Why are they included? Most of these sections focus on (real and imagined) women. How do they contribute to the book's mission to provide a humanizing portrait of the so-called "psycho girlfriend"? Where else in the book does this implicit theme of asymmetrical or stereotypical gender roles appear? Does *Girl in Need of a Tourniquet* effectively draw attention to Borderline Personality "as a lens," in Dana Becker's words, "that amplifies the self-defeating qualities of normal femininity"?

3. Johnson characterizes her relationship with her mother as the original romantic attachment. Assuming that the statement is not intended to be literal, what might the author mean when she says she is trying as a young girl to "seduce" her mother?

4. In an early chapter called "Attachment Thief," Johnson describes her mother's appeal as "red miniskirt fire." What does this image convey about her mother? What does Lisa agree to help her father steal from her mother? Why does the author use such densely symbolic language at this point in the story? What happens when she leaves her mother and this fire behind? How does this fable explain her behavioral patterns as an adult?

5. Discuss the role of the father in the book. Is Johnson able to refrain from assigning the label of all good or all bad in the portrait of her father? In the earliest drafts of *Girl in Need of a Tourniquet*, the narrative focused narrowly on mother-daughter dynamics. What do the sections on father-daughter dynamics add to the story of Lisa's adult romantic relationships?

6. Johnson describes the writing process for *Girl in Need of a Tourniquet* as slow, frustrating, tedious, and off-base at first, but eventually turning into something easier, something more fun, more honest, and more open-ended. The book finally came together when she stopped trying to force it to fit the usual cultural narratives about family psychology, romantic love, moral reasoning, and self-preservation. No matter how hard she tried, she could not get *Girl in Need of a Tourniquet* to be or say what she expected. How does the story surprise her? What does she discover about herself that she did not already know when she first started writing it? What elements of mystery shape the narrative? What surprised you most as you read the book?

7. Borderline Personality Disorder is a highly controversial diagnosis in contemporary U.S. American culture, criticized for being vague, for carrying stigma, for being applied disproportionately to women than to men, and for being used as shorthand by therapists and nurses for individuals who are considered "difficult" or perceived as "manipulative" and "self-absorbed." How does Lisa react to the label when she

first encounters it in therapy? Do the details of Lisa's personal history support a diagnosis of Borderline Personality Disorder?

8. What does Johnson mean when she groups the labels of BORDERLINE, HYSTERIC, and LESBIAN together and calls them dead stars or smears of light? What do the words have in common? Is there anything about the coming out story (becoming lesbian) that resembles the story of coming to terms with her diagnosis (becoming borderline)?

9. Discuss the author's choice to omit the word "disorder" from the book's title. How significant is word choice—Borderline Personality Disorder vs. attachment disorder—in naming this condition? If the DSM-V replaces the current label with the proposed term, *Emotion Regulation Disorder,* or moves the diagnosis from Axis II to Axis I, how would these revisions to professional psychiatric protocol impact the individual experience or public image of the condition? Do you recognize yourself or anyone you know in the various descriptions, typologies, and diagrams of Borderline Personality included in *Girl in Need of a Tourniquet?* What are the benefits and disadvantages of positioning this disorder on a continuum of perceptions and behaviors with no clear line separating those who have Borderline Personality from those who just tend to have a hard time with relationships?

10. After her divorce at age 20, Lisa went into a long depression she says she "misrecognized as missing [her] ex." What was the deeper

source of her depression? What other emotions does Lisa incorrectly identify during her adolescence and first decade of adulthood? What attitudes does she express toward love, grief, and other powerful feelings? What role do emotion phobia, emotional illiteracy, and the therapeutic labor toward emotional integration play in *Girl in Need of a Tourniquet*? How is therapy the subtext of the book?

11. Autobiographical narratives typically include two versions of the author—the foolish younger self as protagonist and the older wiser narrator/author who reflects on her former self for the benefit of readers who might learn from the author's mistakes and mishaps— but *Girl in Need of a Tourniquet* complicates this form in several ways. Where, why, and to what effect does the author depart from the traditional linear progress towards maturity and mental wellness? Where, why, and to what effect does Johnson blur the lines between the young fool and the insightful or experienced narrator? How does Johnson use her own stubborn obliviousness in the service of illuminating Borderline Personality for the reader?

12. Some of the most grueling passages in *Girl in Need of a Tourniquet* recount scenes of self-cutting. Many authors of trauma memoirs assert the importance of coming to voice and telling the truth about their lives as a crucial turning point with a healing effect that detoxifies suppressed memories. Some social critics extend the claim of a curative effect beyond the author to the reader as taboo

or unspeakable experiences are transferred from the realm of the secret, the stigmatized, and the shameful to the public sphere where they become visible as shared symptoms resulting from fairly logical psychological, social, and biological causes. Still others express caution and concern about such narratives, warning that images of self-cutting can trigger a self-injurious episode in vulnerable readers. Weigh these claims against each other in the context of Johnson's memoir. Are the scenes important to the narrative? Are they honest? Hostile? How did they affect your reading experience? How do they relate to the title of the book, and to its representation of the borderline as an "emotional hemophiliac"?

13. Say there are many different versions of *Girl in Need of a Tourniquet* depending on who the reader is. What is the book's message for other borderlines? For nonborderline family members, romantic partners, and close friends—often inelegantly called nons—of borderlines? For social workers, school guidance counselors, clinical therapists, and psychiatrists? For feminist literary critics who specialize in women's autobiography or in gendered representations of madness? For disability theorists? For other late-blooming lesbians-after-marriage?

14. The title of the book comes from a line in a song by Aimee Mann. Music is a cultural outlet saturated with painful emotions, self-destructive patterns, and misguided fantasies of rescue. Some of the most poignant songs draw their gravitational force from the

confusion of healthy love with the addictive highs of infatuation, or security with the ambiguous pleasures of rivalry, or psychological integration with the precarious search for approval from another person placed in the role of obsessive target or attachment fetish figure. What other song lyrics does Johnson use in *Girl in Need of a Tourniquet* to reveal personal psychological themes? What accounts for the prominent theme in music of lost or unrequited love and the bragging rights of reckless nihilistic abandon? Is the music industry overpopulated by borderlines? Is popular music intrinsically borderline? What songs played a significant role in your romantic history? Is it productive to let off steam by listening to songs of loss, distress, rage, or euphoric infatuation, or is this outlet used more for emotional self-cutting than catharsis?

15. Discuss the final scene of the book. What is the author's tone in the last few pages? If you were a fortune-teller, what would you predict happens next in the lives of the residents at the Haney-Johnson Halfway House for the Bright but Broken-Hearted? If you were a counselor, what advice would you give Lisa? Or to Stace? Or to Jay?

ABOUT THE AUTHOR

© LES DUGGINS

MERRI LISA JOHNSON believes in bold lines, strange truths, off rhymes, and the art of the glimpse. After pursuing various graduate degrees in colder climates, Johnson returned to the U.S. southeast where she performs a curious balancing act as author, professor, and Women's and Gender Studies program administrator. A newlywed lesbian-after-marriage, Johnson currently resides in South Carolina with her partner Stace and their two loyal shih tzus. Johnson's previous publications include three anthologies in feminist cultural studies—*Jane Sexes It Up: True Confessions of Feminist Desire, Flesh for Fantasy: Producing and Consuming Exotic Dance* (with R. Danielle Egan and Katherine Frank), and *Third Wave Feminism and Television: Jane Puts It in a Box*—as well as essays published in *Sex and Single Girls: Women Write on Sexuality, Herspace: Women, Writing, and Solitude, Homewrecker: An Adultery Reader,* and *Fucking Daphne: Mostly True Stories and Fictions.*

SELECTED TITLES FROM SEAL PRESS

For more than thirty years, Seal Press has published groundbreaking books. By women. For women. Visit our website at www.sealpress.com. Check out the Seal Press blog at www.sealpress.com/blog.

She Bets Her Life: The True Story of a Gambling Addict and the Women Who Saved Her Life, by Mary Sojourner. $17.95, 978-1-58005-298-6. One woman's account of her personal struggle with gambling addiction, this is a hard-hitting confession of the journey to the bottom—and back up.

Sexual Intimacy for Women: A Guide for Same-Sex Couples, by Glenda Corwin, Ph.D. $16.95, 978-1-58005-303-7. In this prescriptive and poignant book, Glenda Corwin, PhD, helps female couples overcome obstacles to sexual intimacy through her examination of the emotional, physical, and psychological aspects of same-sex relationships.

Purge: Rehab Diaries, by Nicole Johns. $16.95, 978-1-58005-274-0. An honest, detailed account of Nicole Johns' experience in an eating-disorder treatment facility, avoiding the happily-ever-after while offering hope to the millions struggling with eating disorders.

Loaded: Women and Addiction, by Jill Talbot. $14.95, 978-1-58005-218-4. A poignant, gut-wrenching memoir of one woman's complicated relationship with multiple addictions.

Addicted Like Me: A Mother-Daughter Story of Substance Abuse and Recovery, by Karen Franklin and Lauren King. $16.95, 978-1-58005-286-3. A mother and daughter share their candid struggles with addiction— thirty years apart—giving readers insight into how to break the cycle.

Lesbian Couples: A Guide to Creating Healthy Relationships, by D. Merilee Clunis and G. Dorsey Green. $ 16.95, 978-1-58005-131-6. Drawing from a decade of research, this helpful and readable resource covers topics from conflict-resolution to commitment ceremonies, using a variety of examples and problem-solving techniques.